Preface

This book represents my perception of COVID-19, in that, when we believe we are living our bleakest days,
there is so much brightness that still surrounds us.
Please continue to search for it, see it and embrace it.

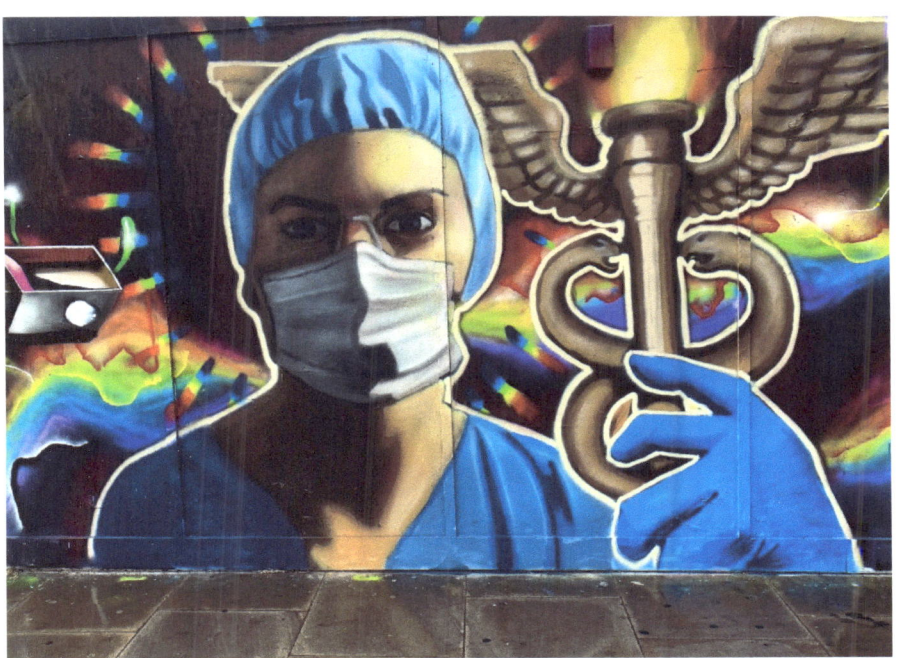

Author: Mrs. Joanna Louise Fox CMgr MCMI
Publisher: Independent Publishing Network
Publication date: October 2020
ISBN: 978-1-83853-855-2

Please direct all enquiries to the author.
Email: info@medi-hr.co.uk
Website: www.medi-hr.co.uk

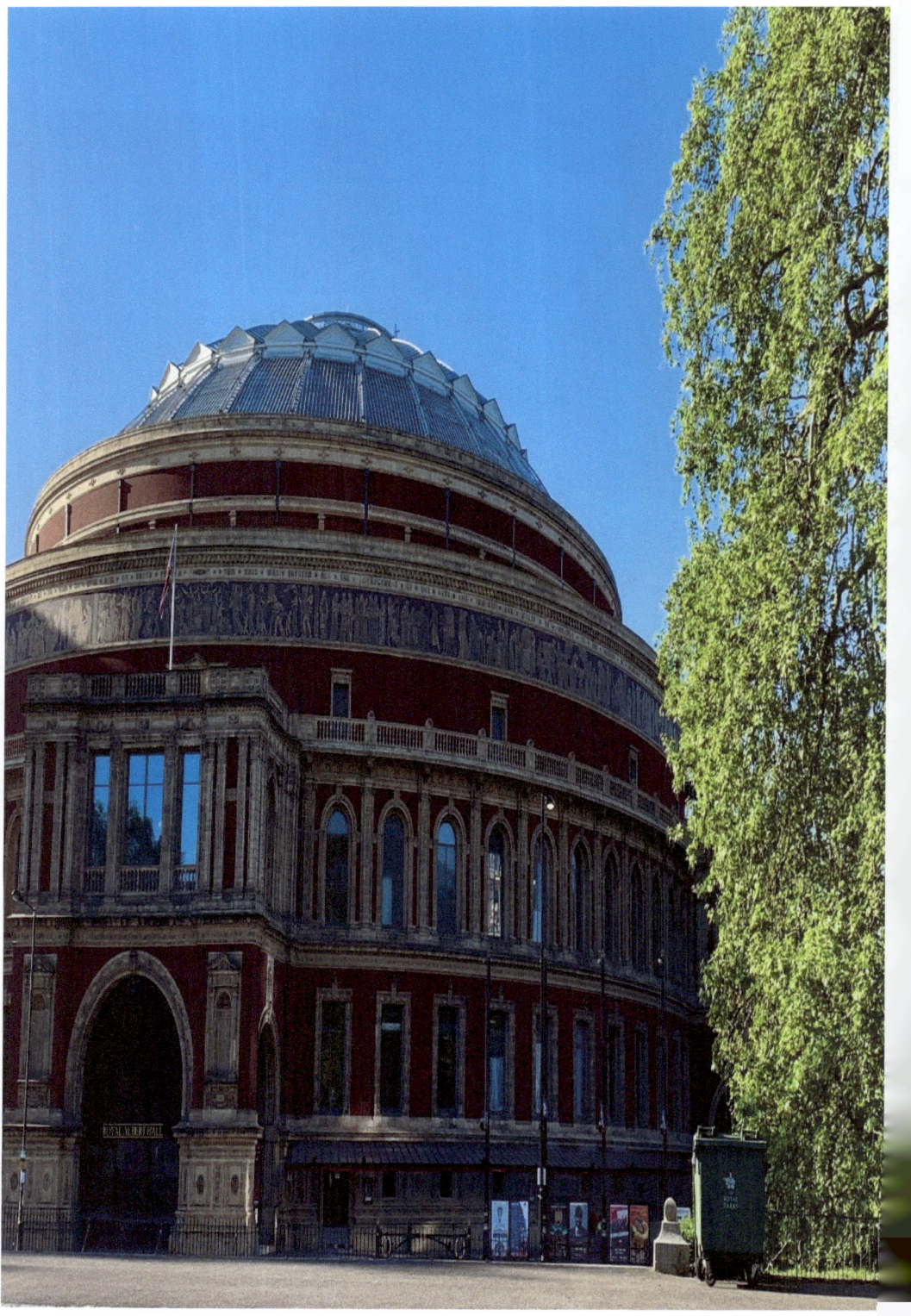

Royal Albert Hall & Albert Memorial

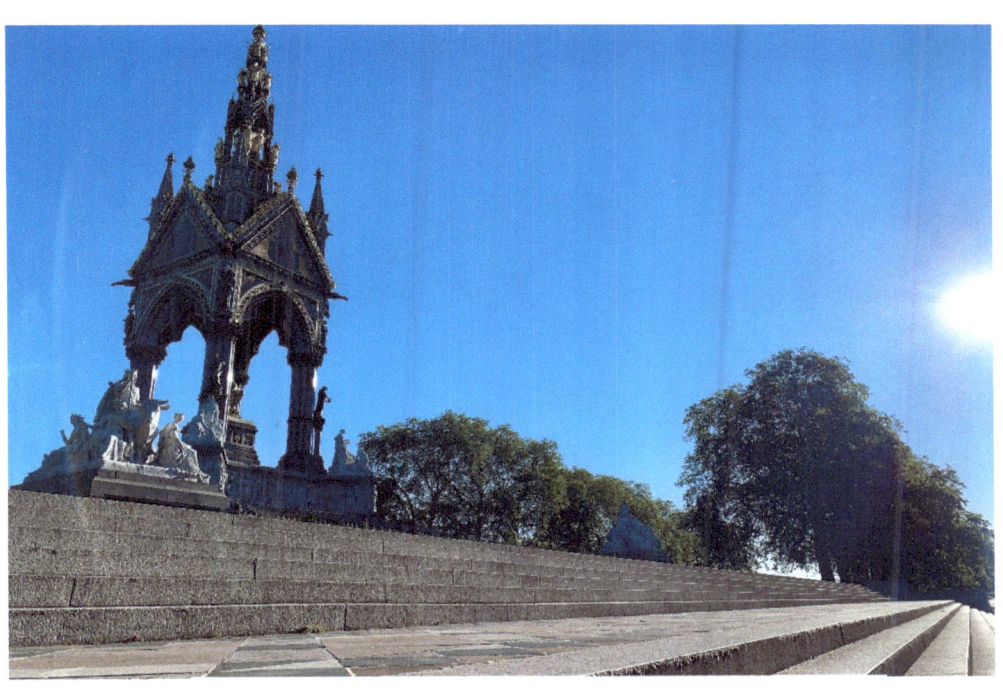

"Turn your face towards the sun
and the shadows will fall behind you"

Trafalgar Square

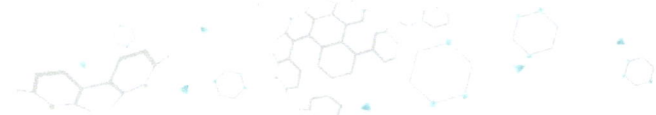

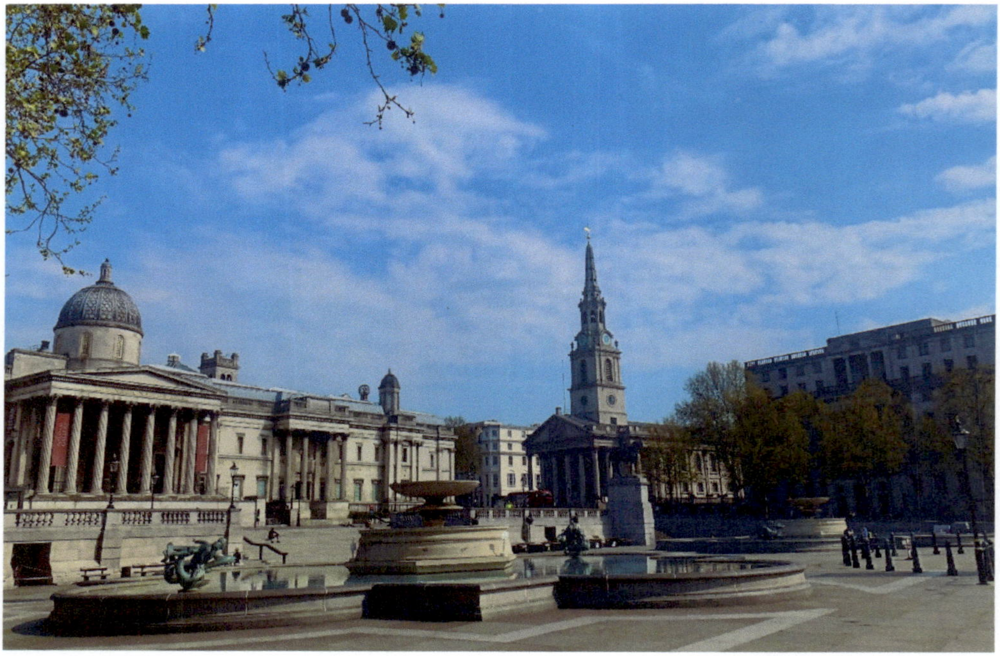

"Positivity will take you far"

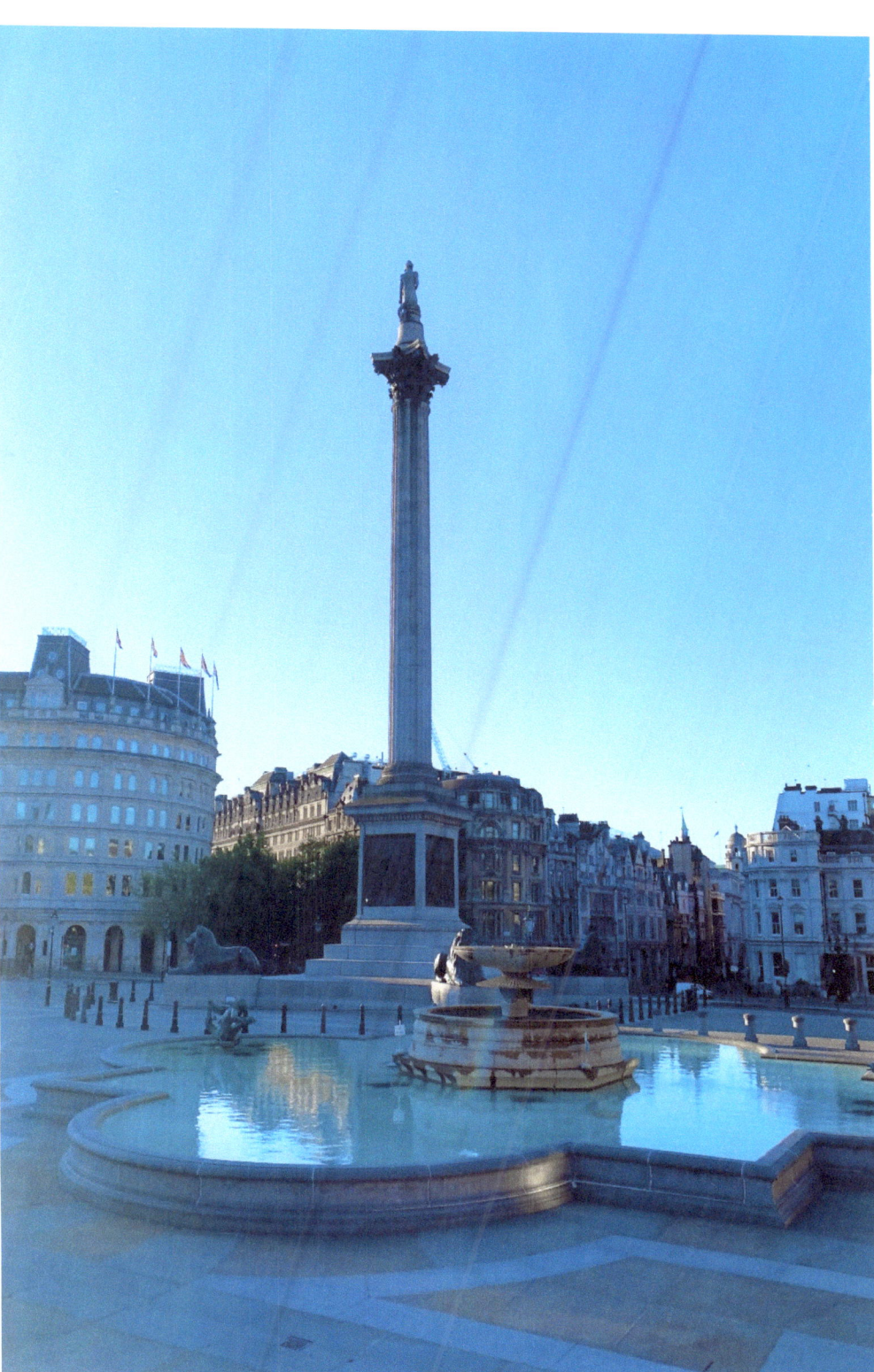

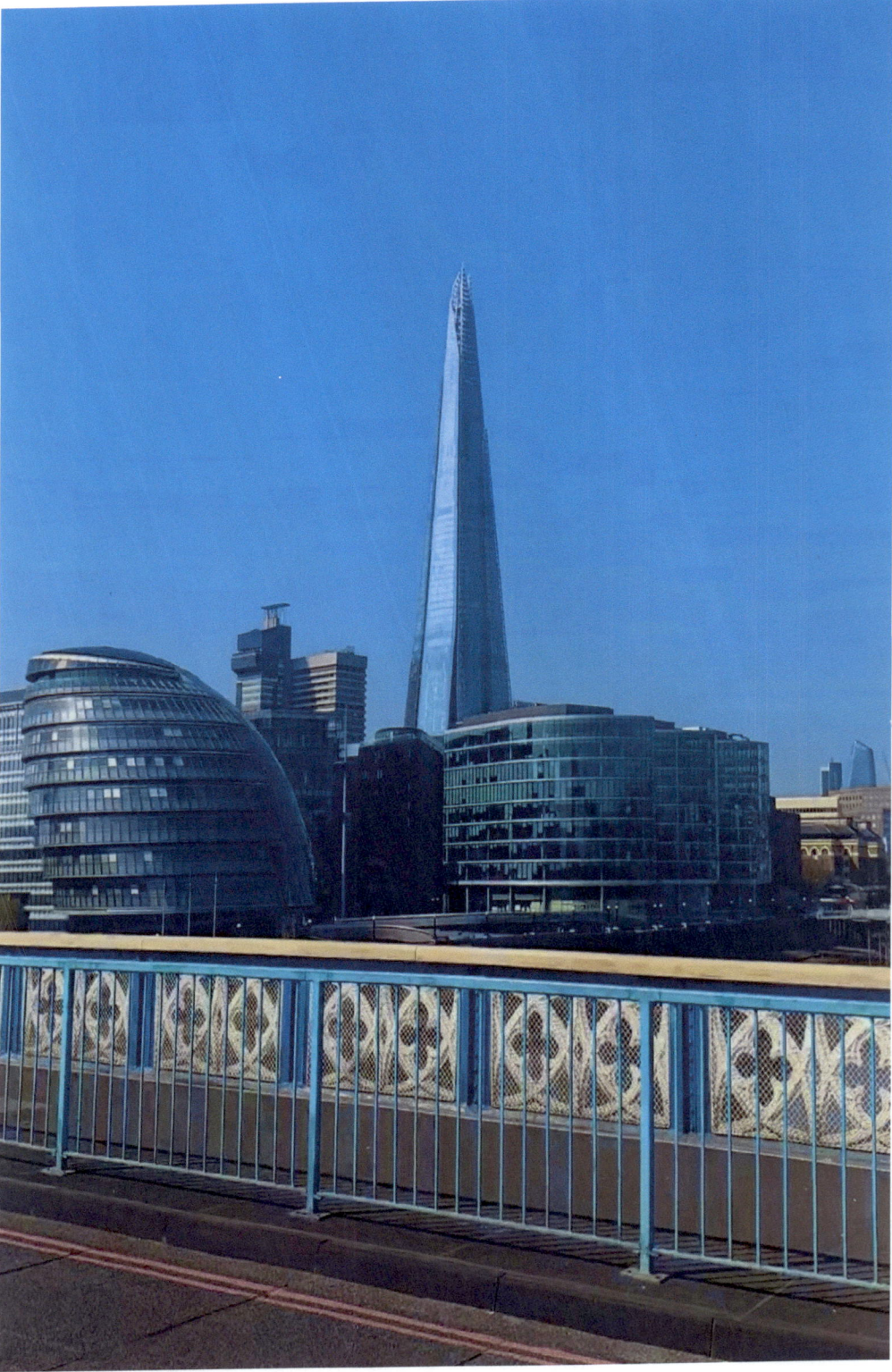

Tower Bridge

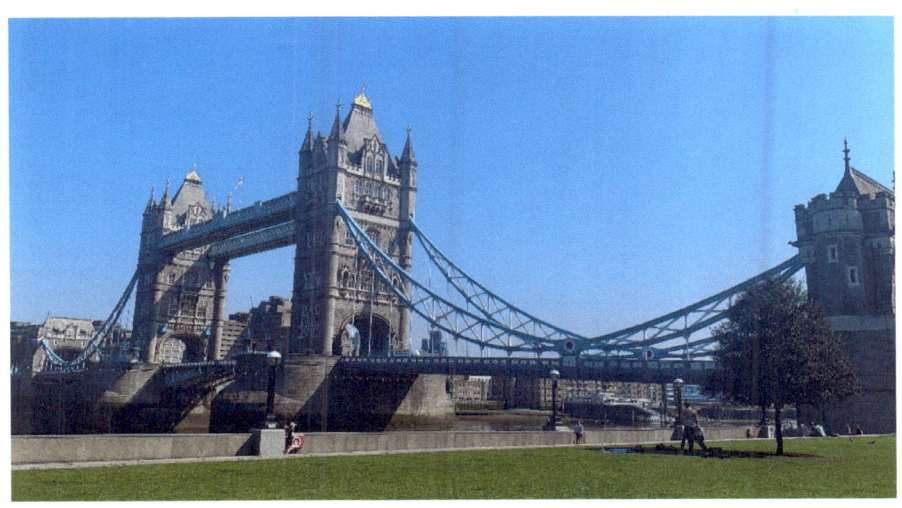

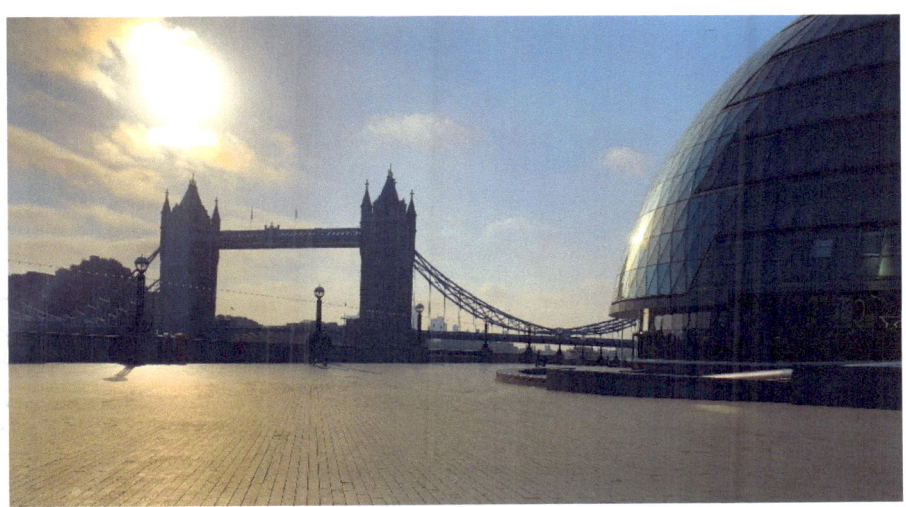

"Perfection is not attainable,
however, excellence it"

Kensington Park

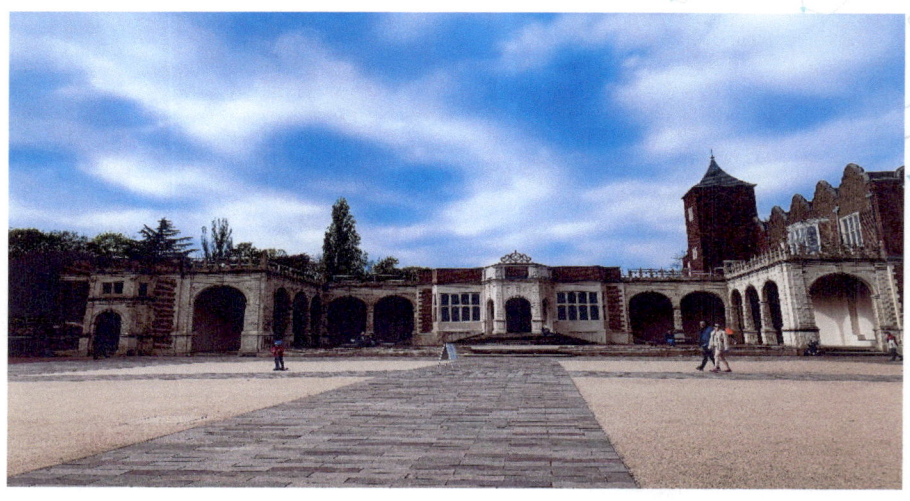

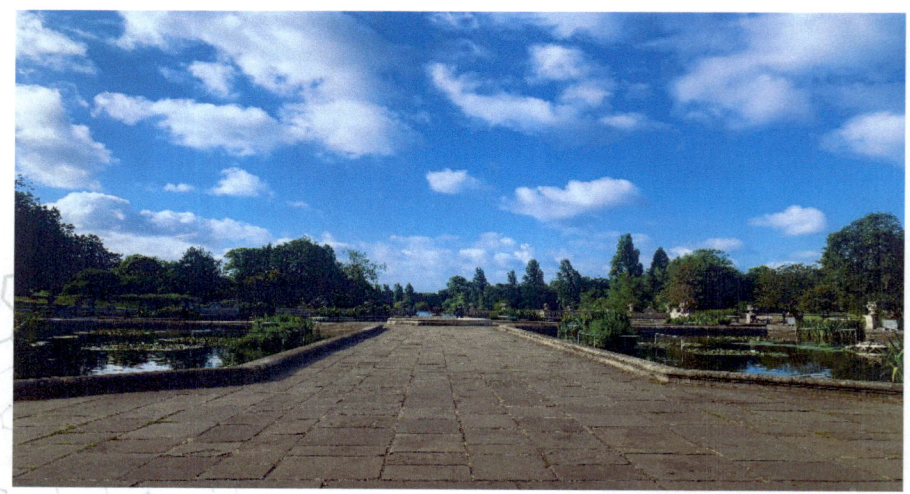

"Pessimism leads to weakness but optimism creates power"

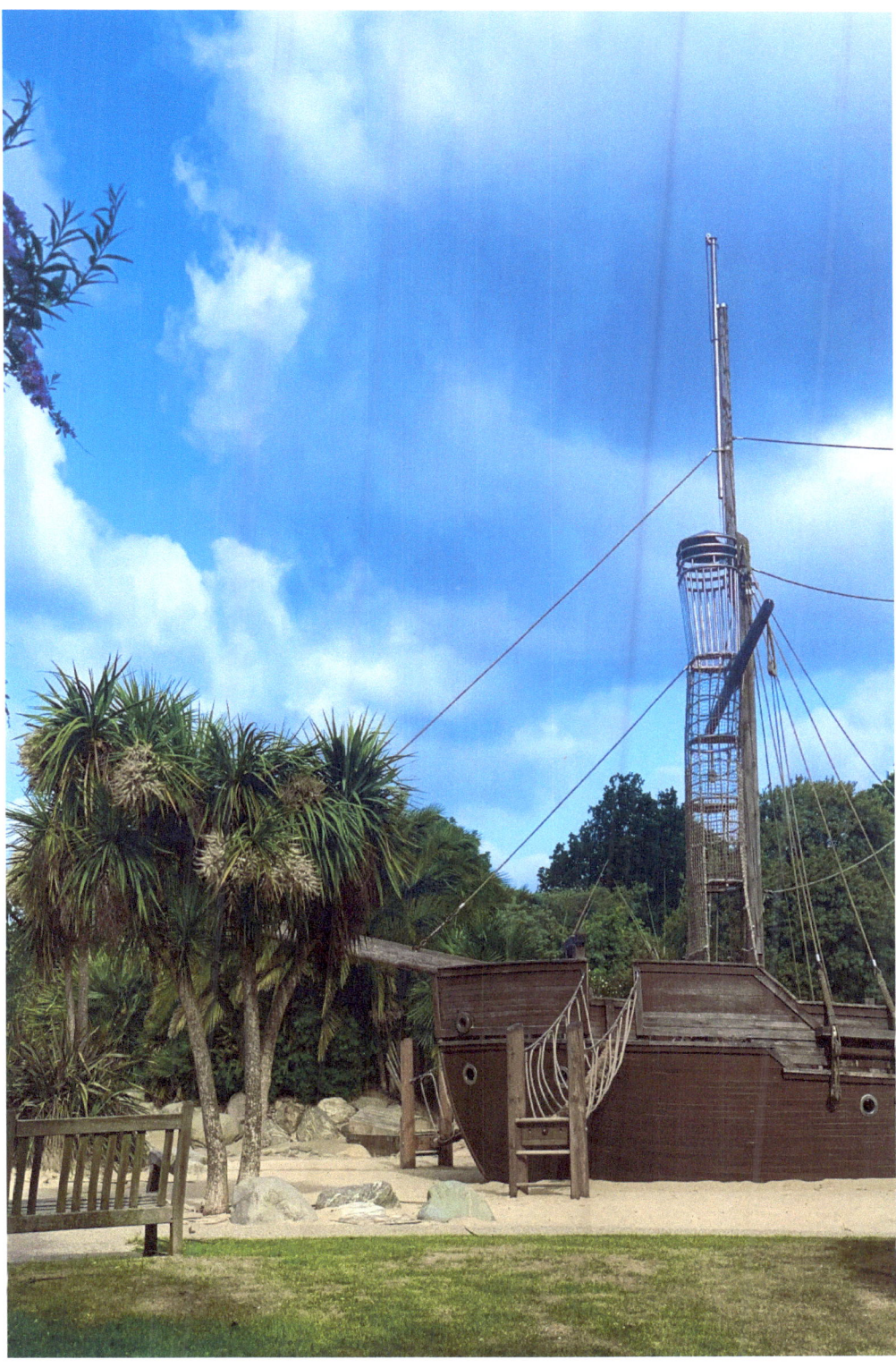

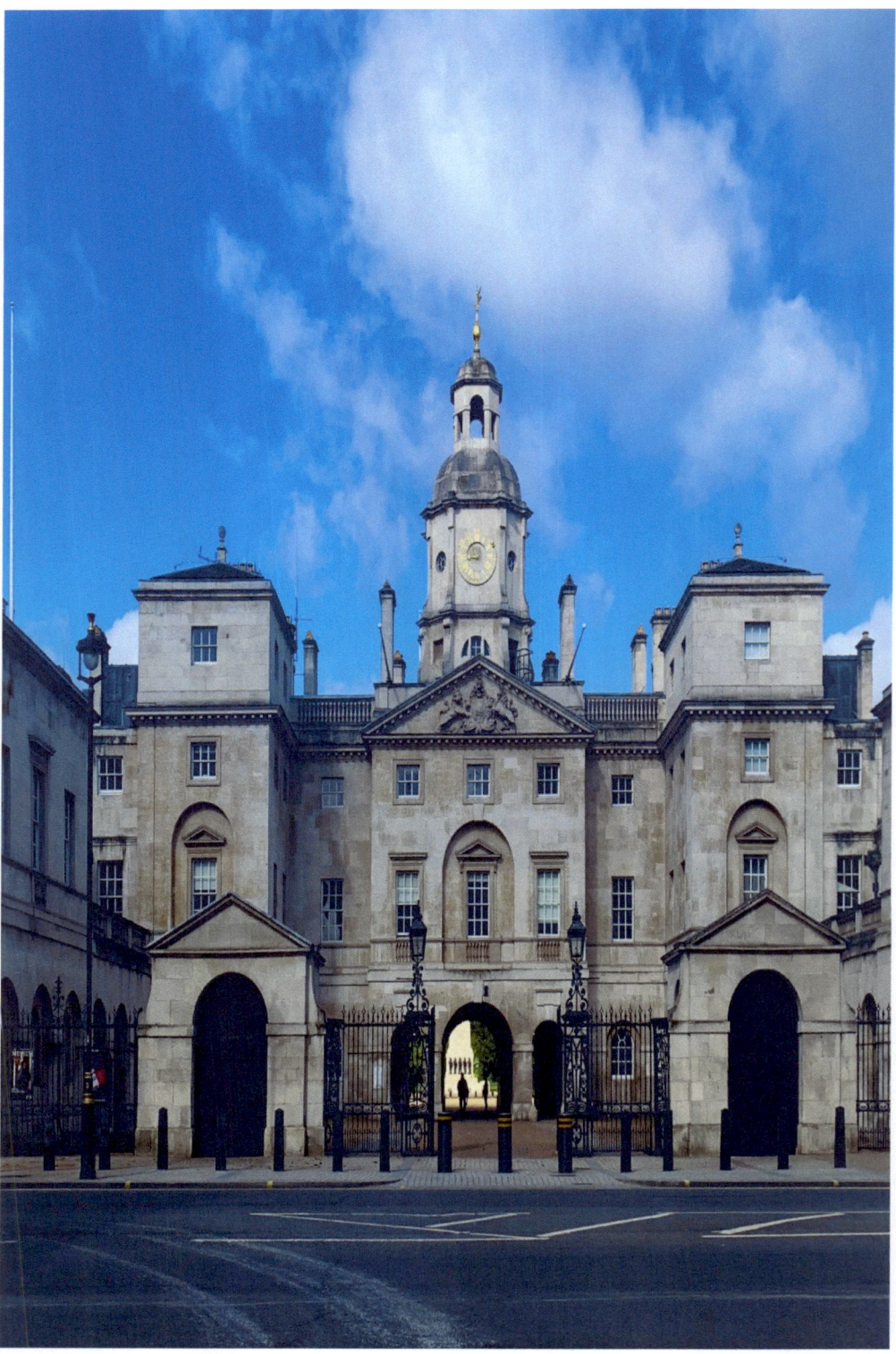

No.10 Downing Street
& Horse Guards Parade

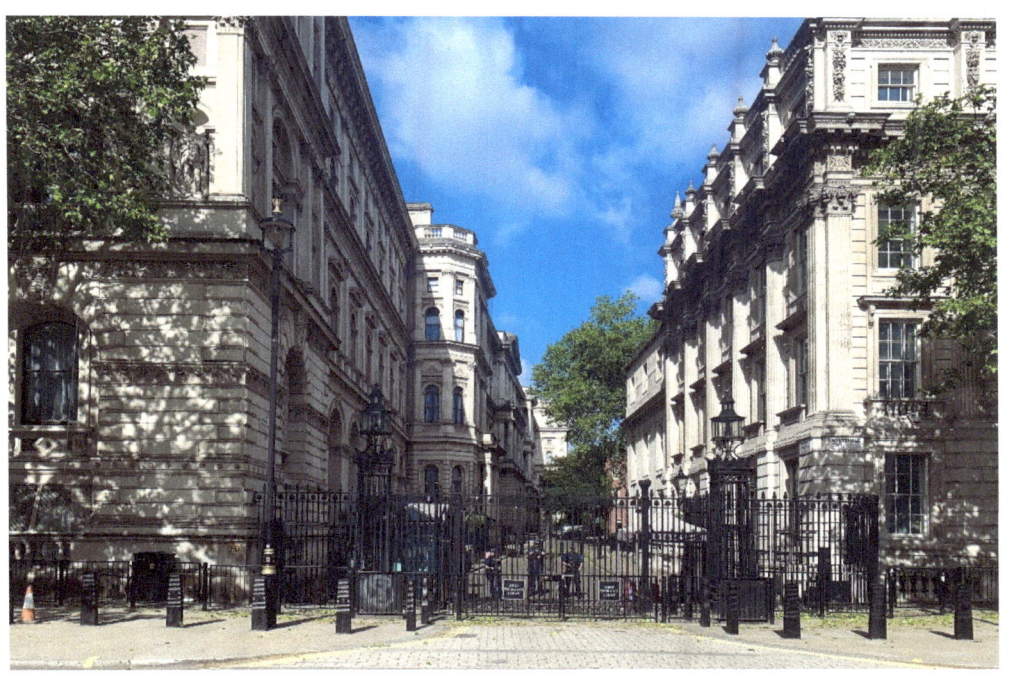

"let your observations shape your thoughts
and not the words of another"

Buckingham Palace & Green Park

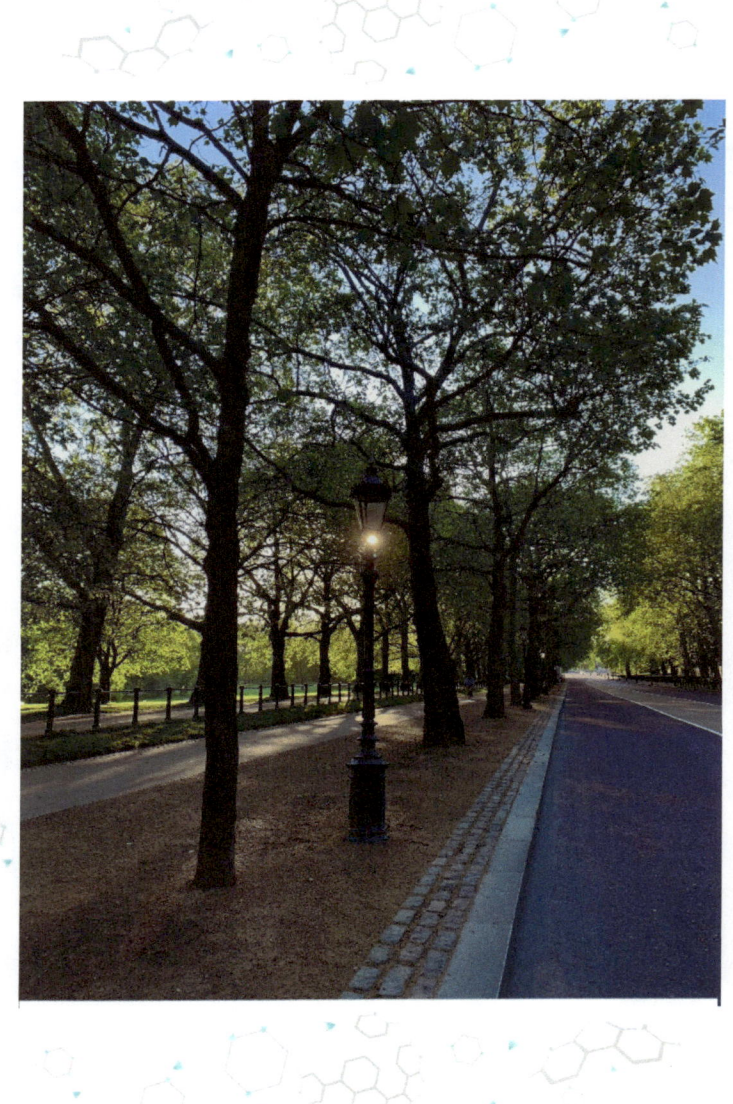

"The streets are not empty; they are filled with the love and the care that we have for each other"

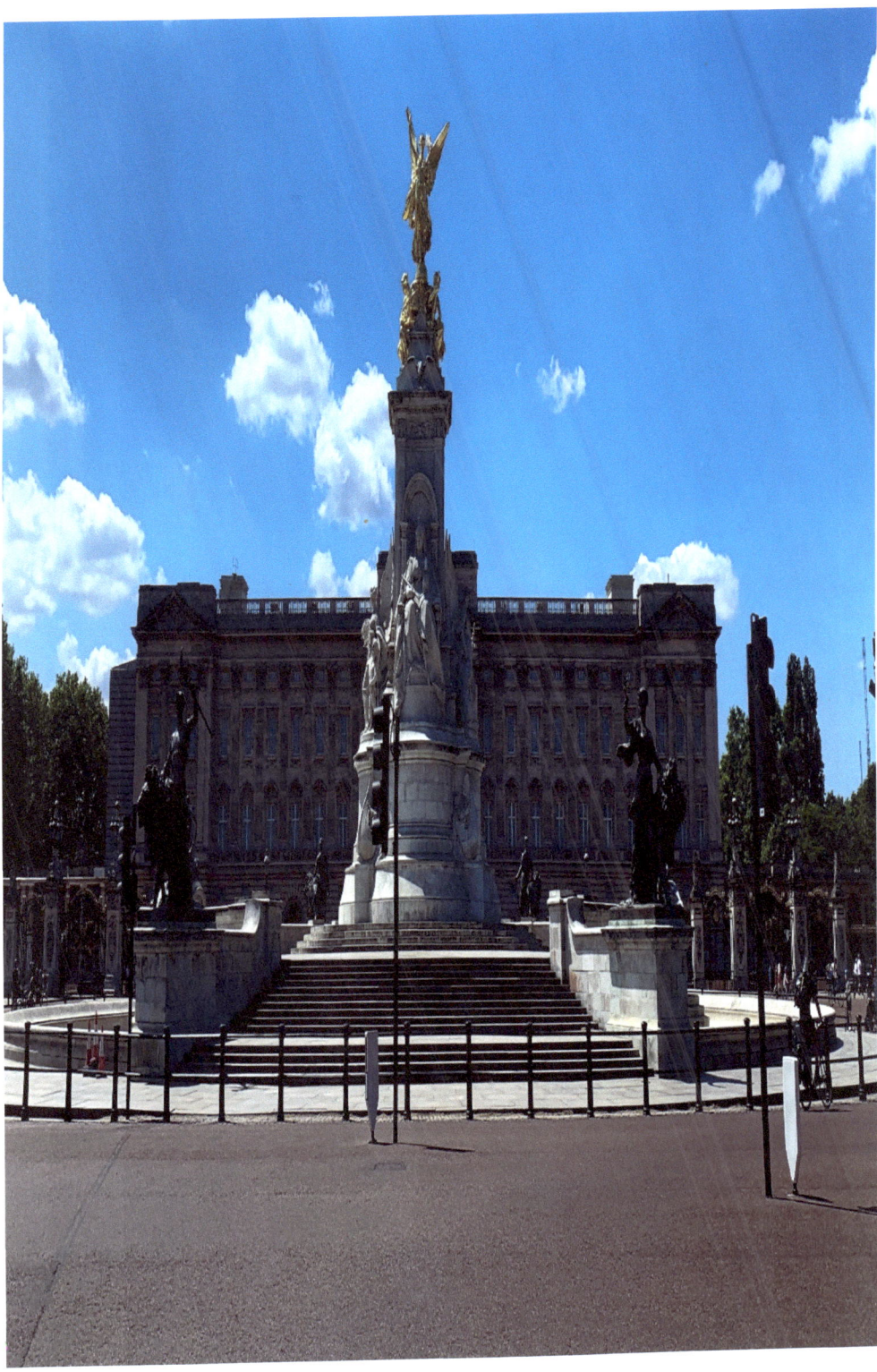

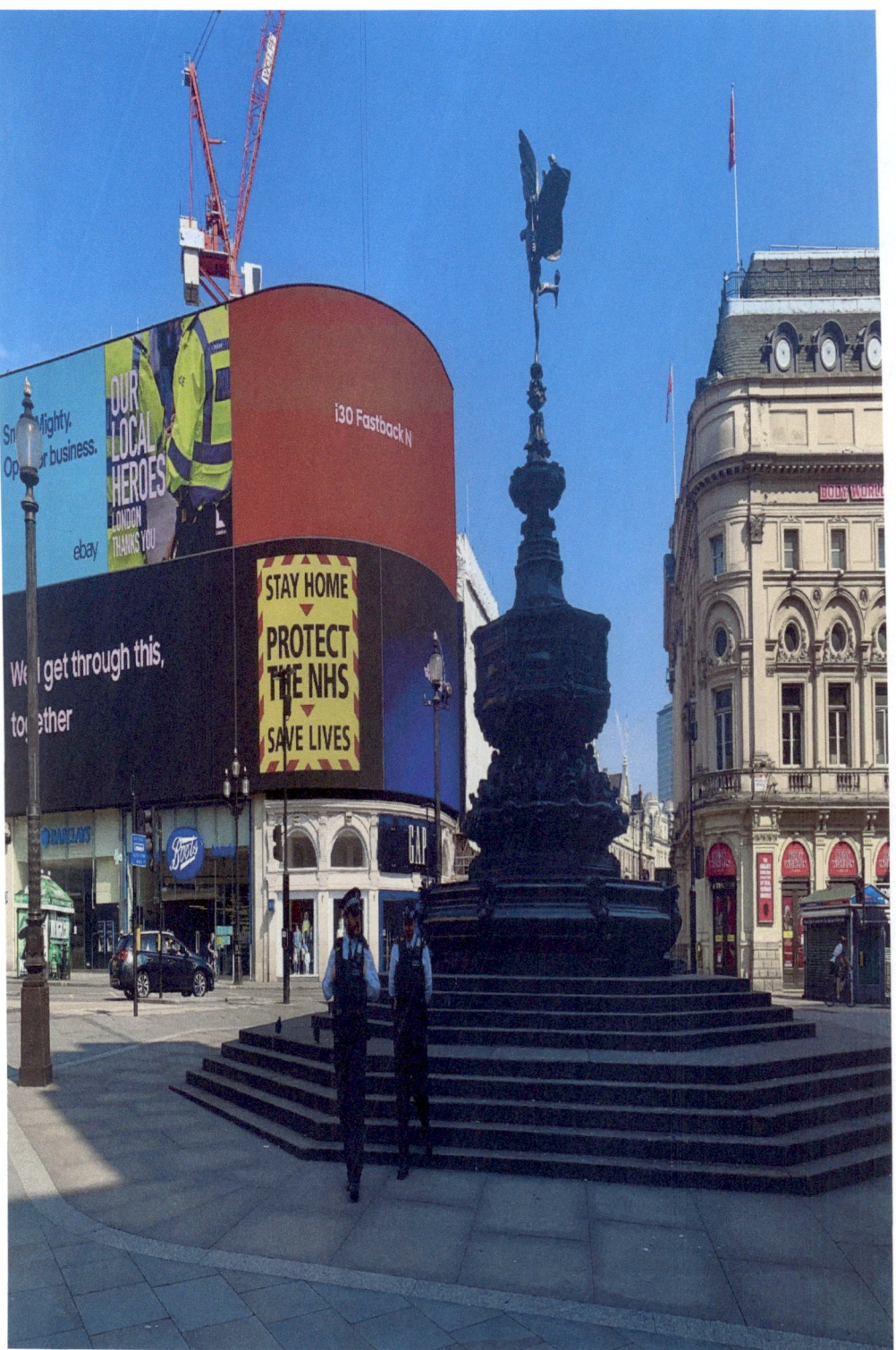

Piccadilly Circus

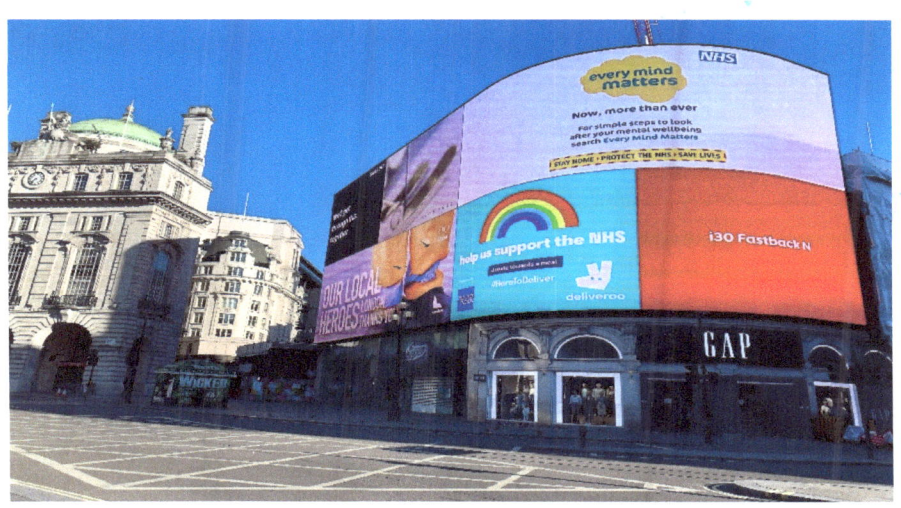

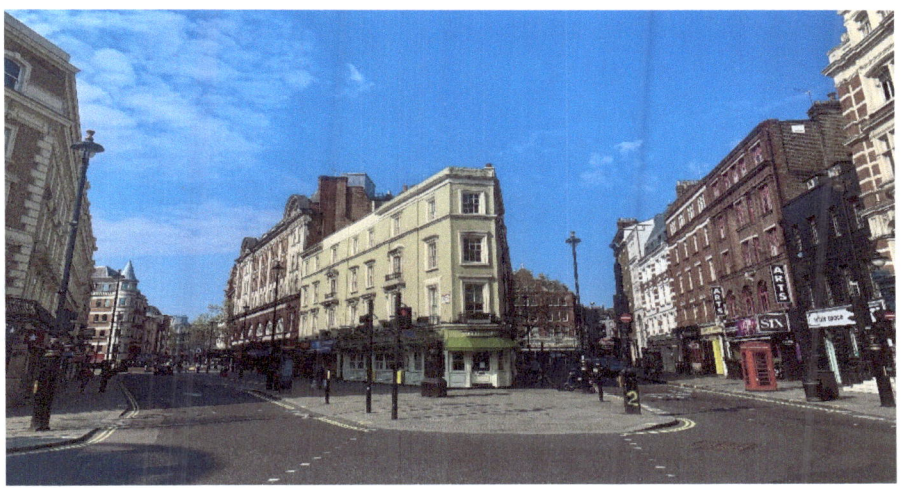

"When you think they took the elevator to success,
the reality is that they climbed a lot of stairs"

Oxford Street & Regent Street

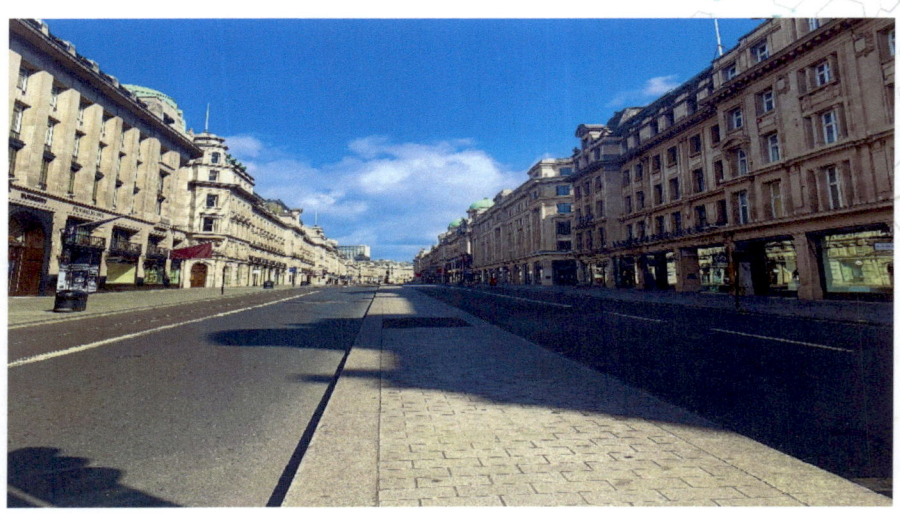

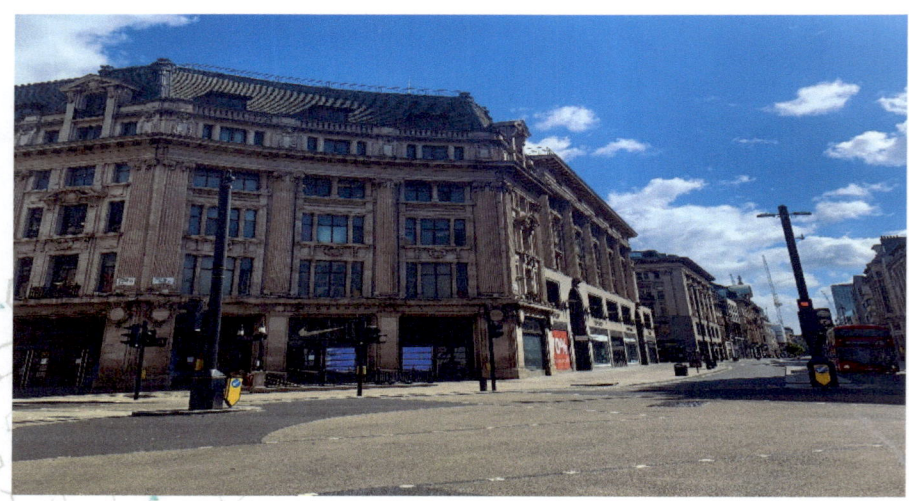

"You do not gain a positive life from that of a negative mind"

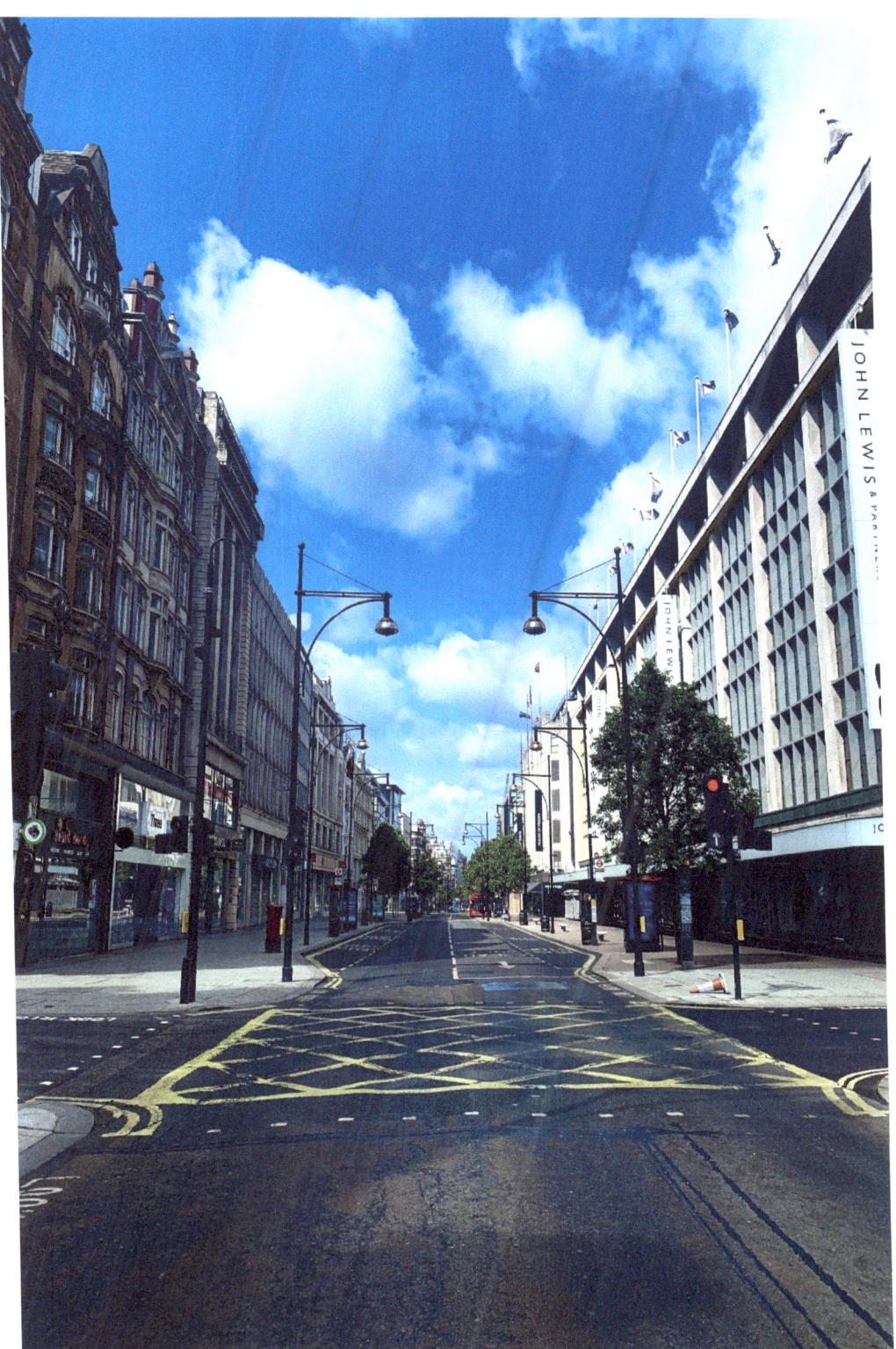

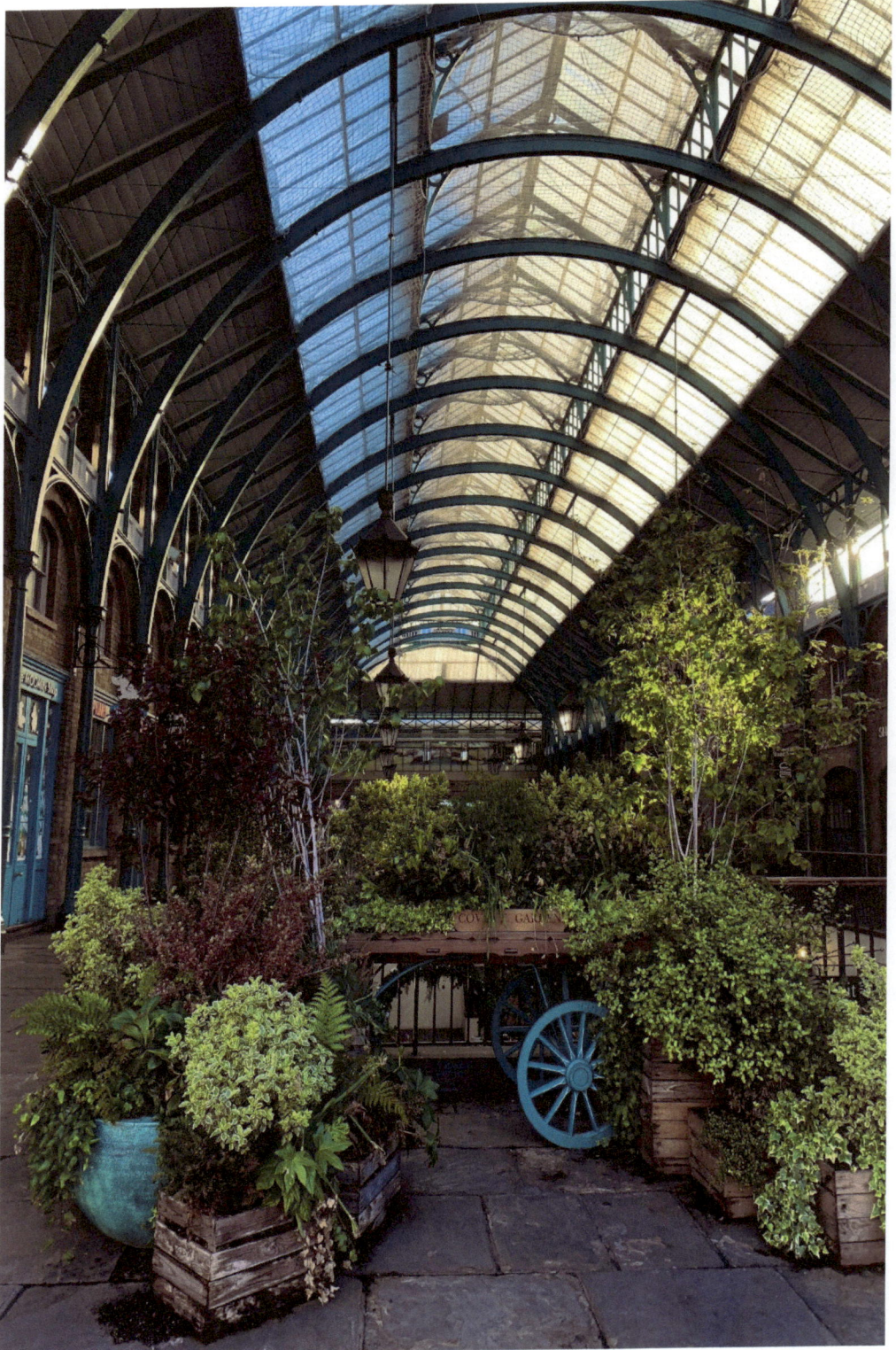

Covent Garden

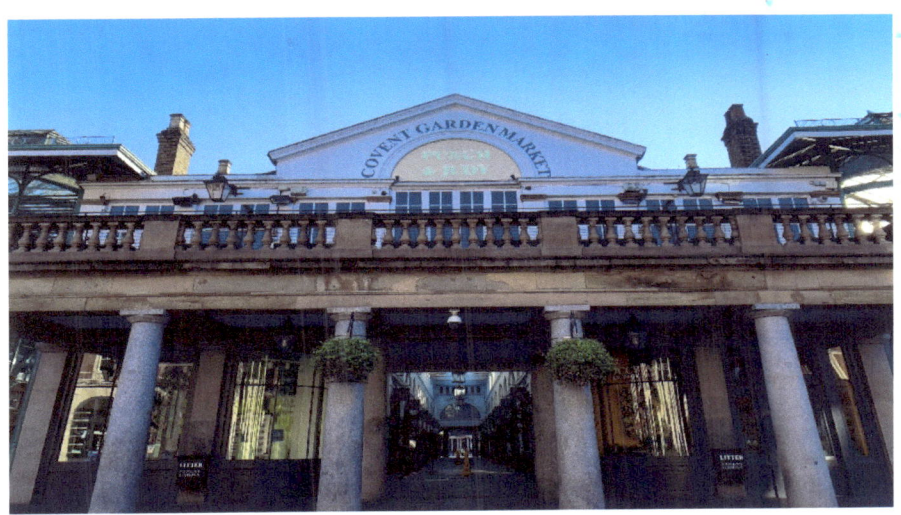

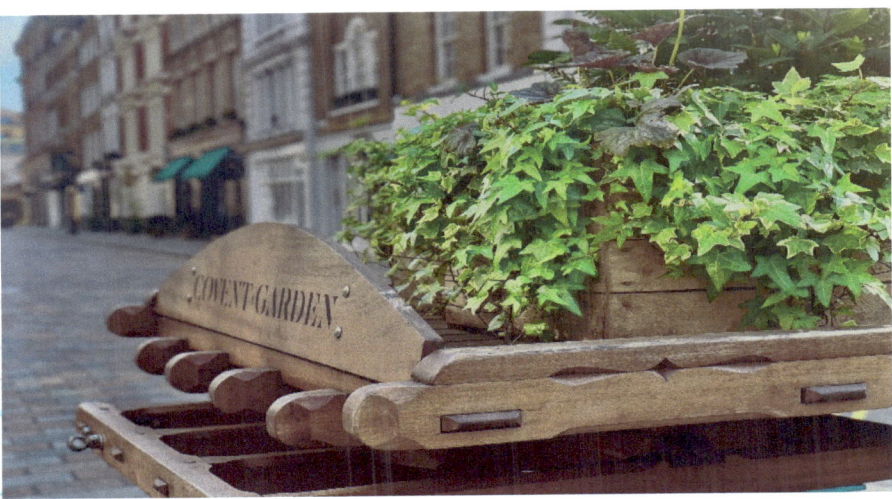

"Yesterday is not ours to recover,
but tomorrow is ours to win or lose"

Leicester Square

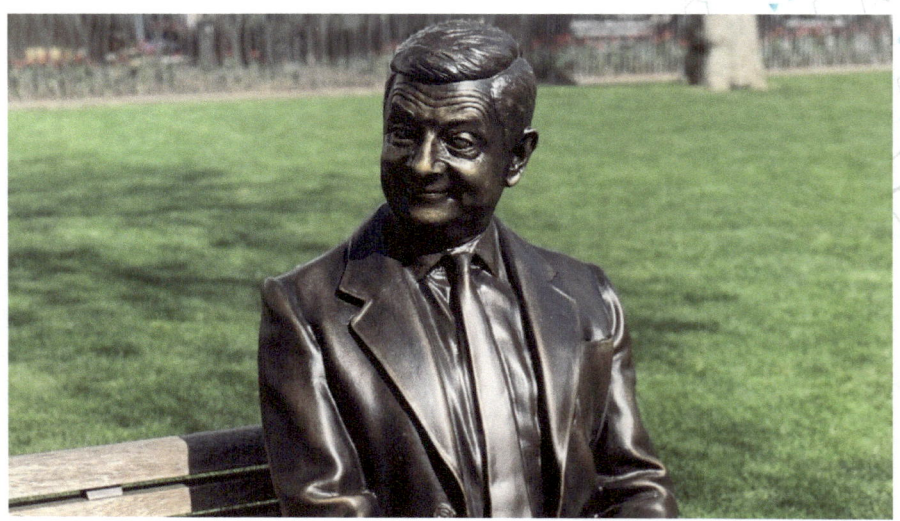

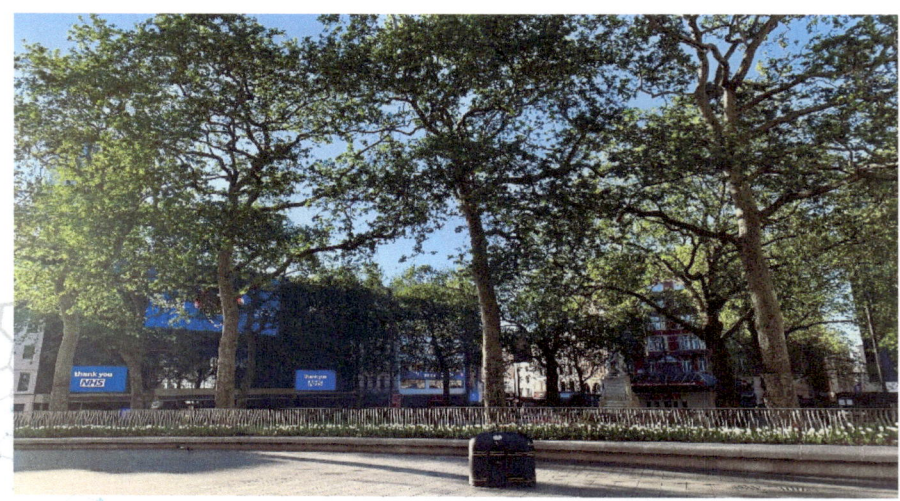

"If you are not making mistakes,
then you're not making progress"

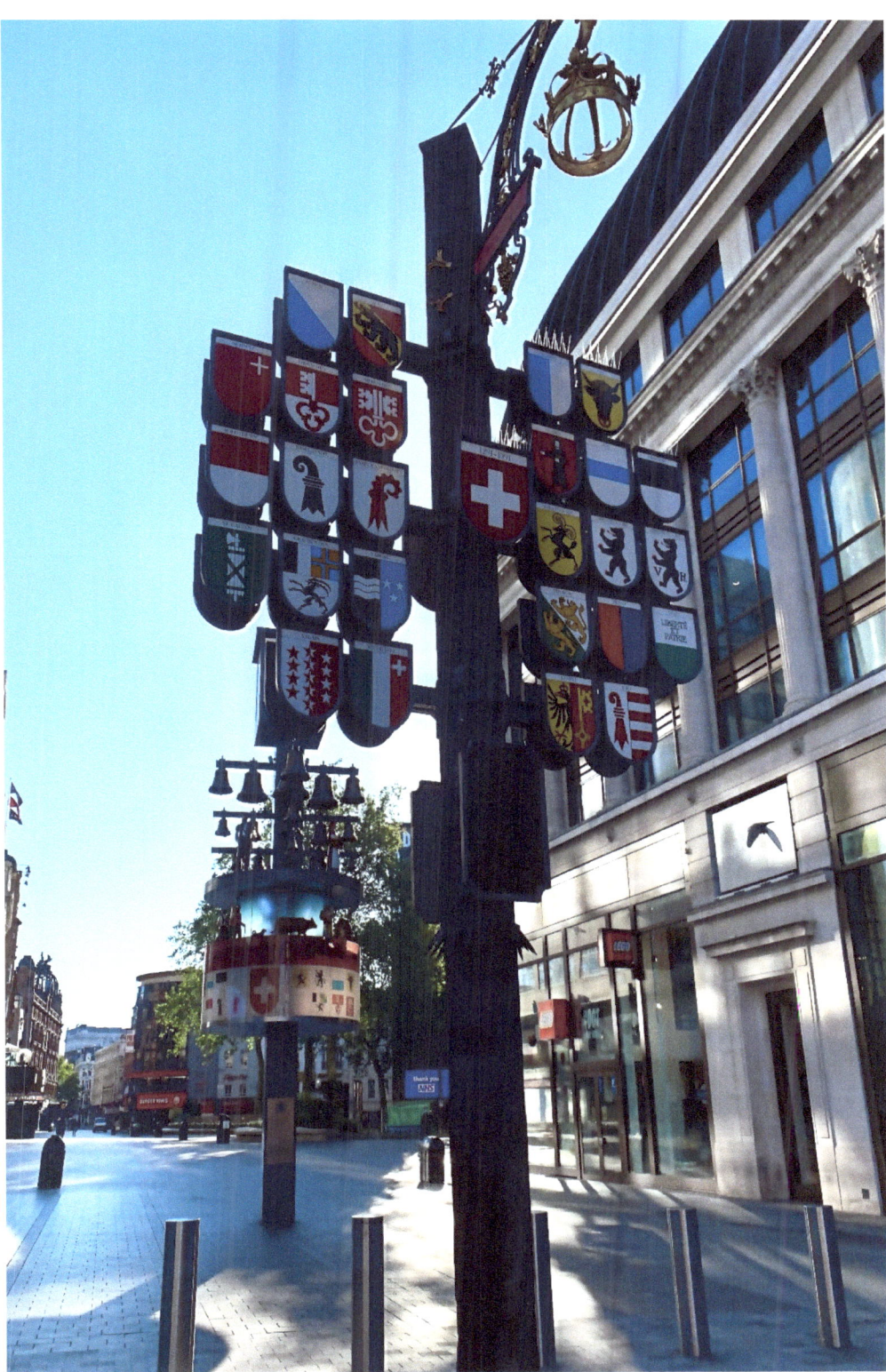

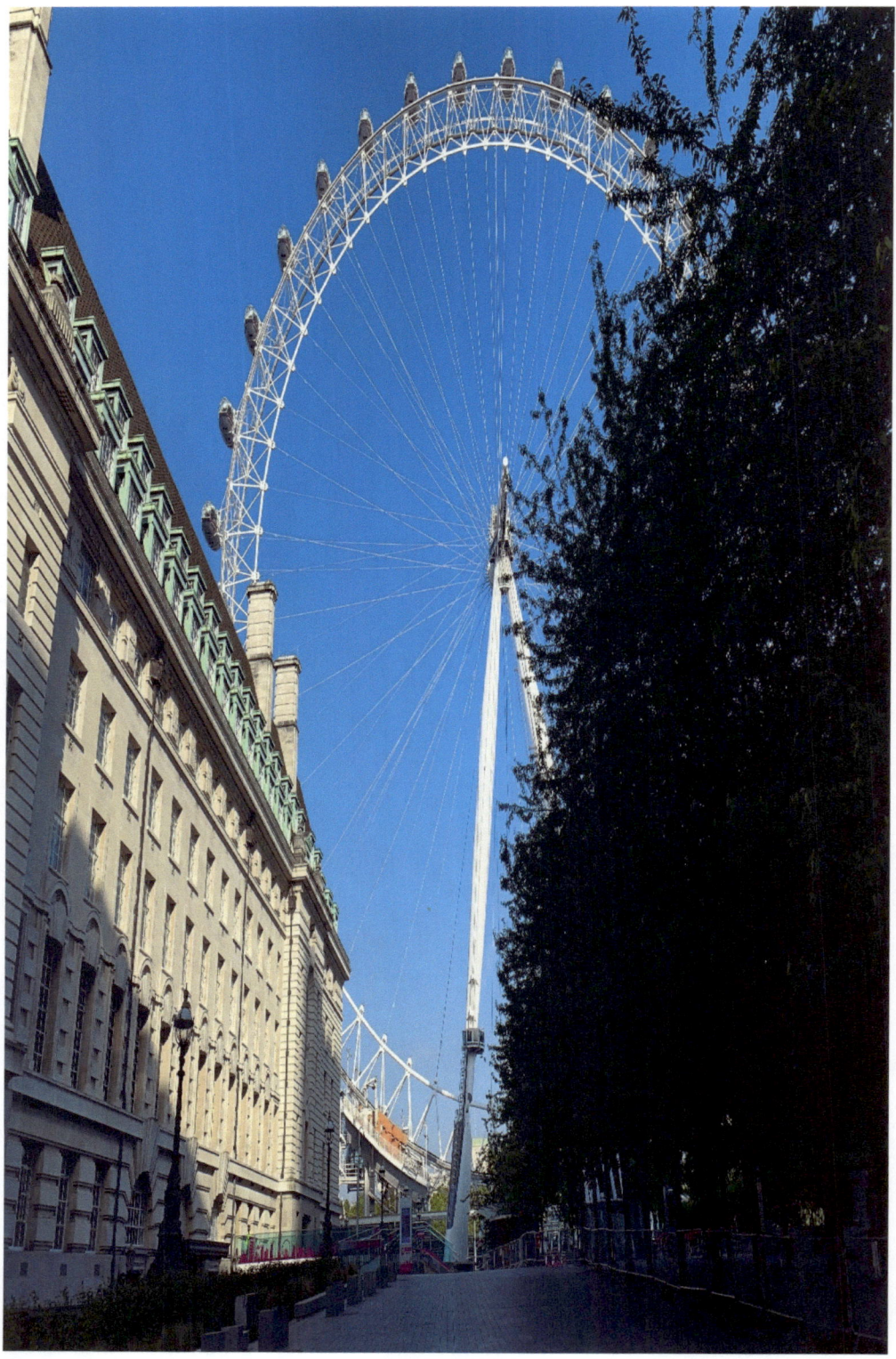

London Eye

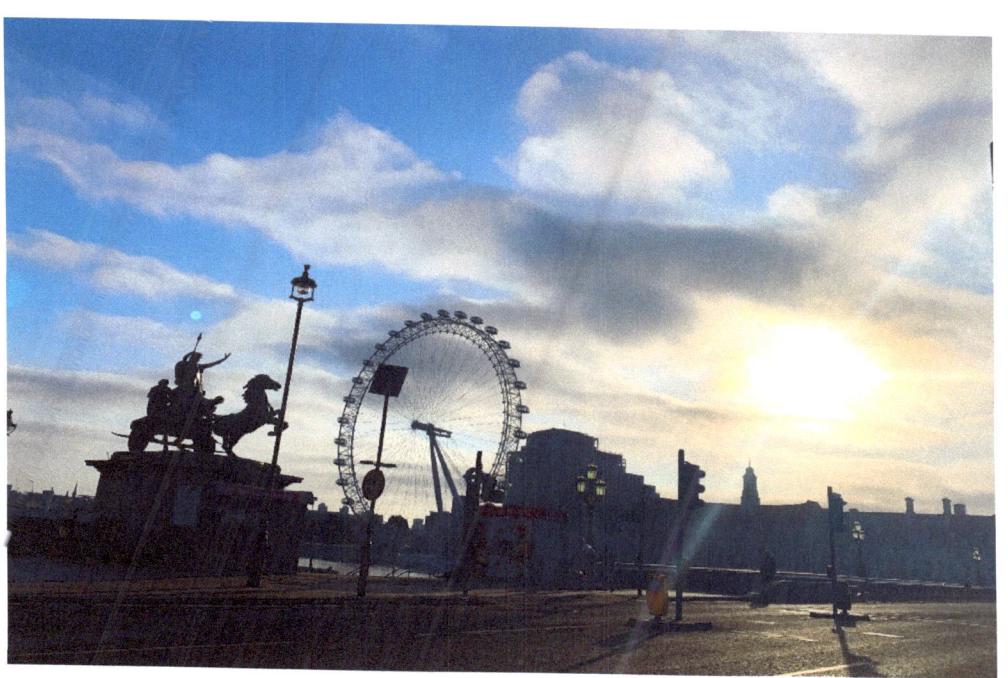

"Correction can do much,
Compliments achieve much more"

China Town & Neal's Yard

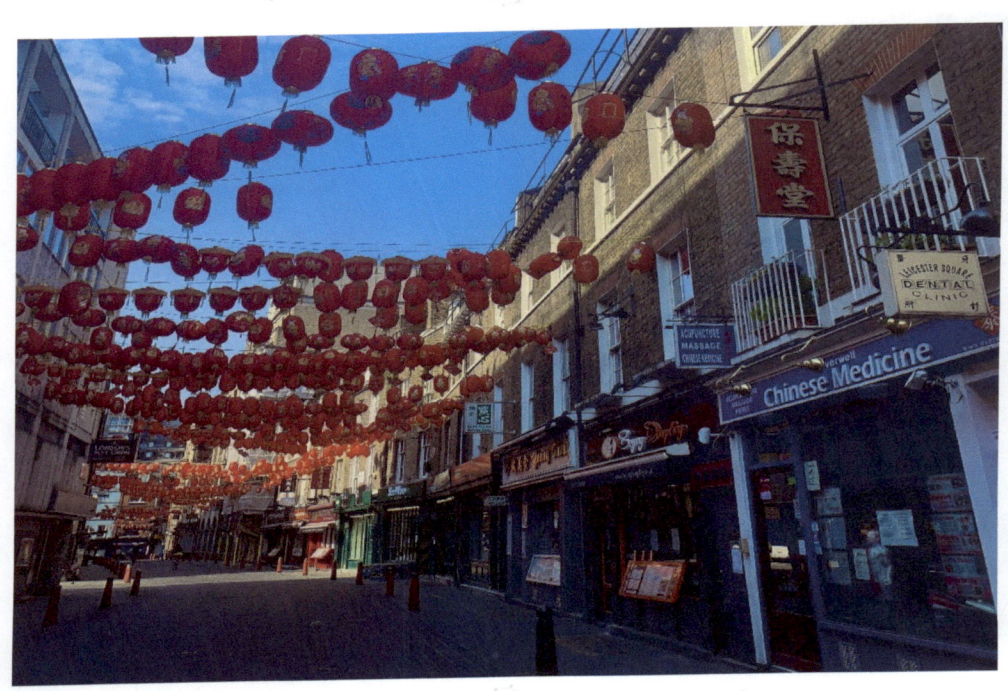

"Laughter can bring sunshine into your home,
even on the most dull, rainy days"

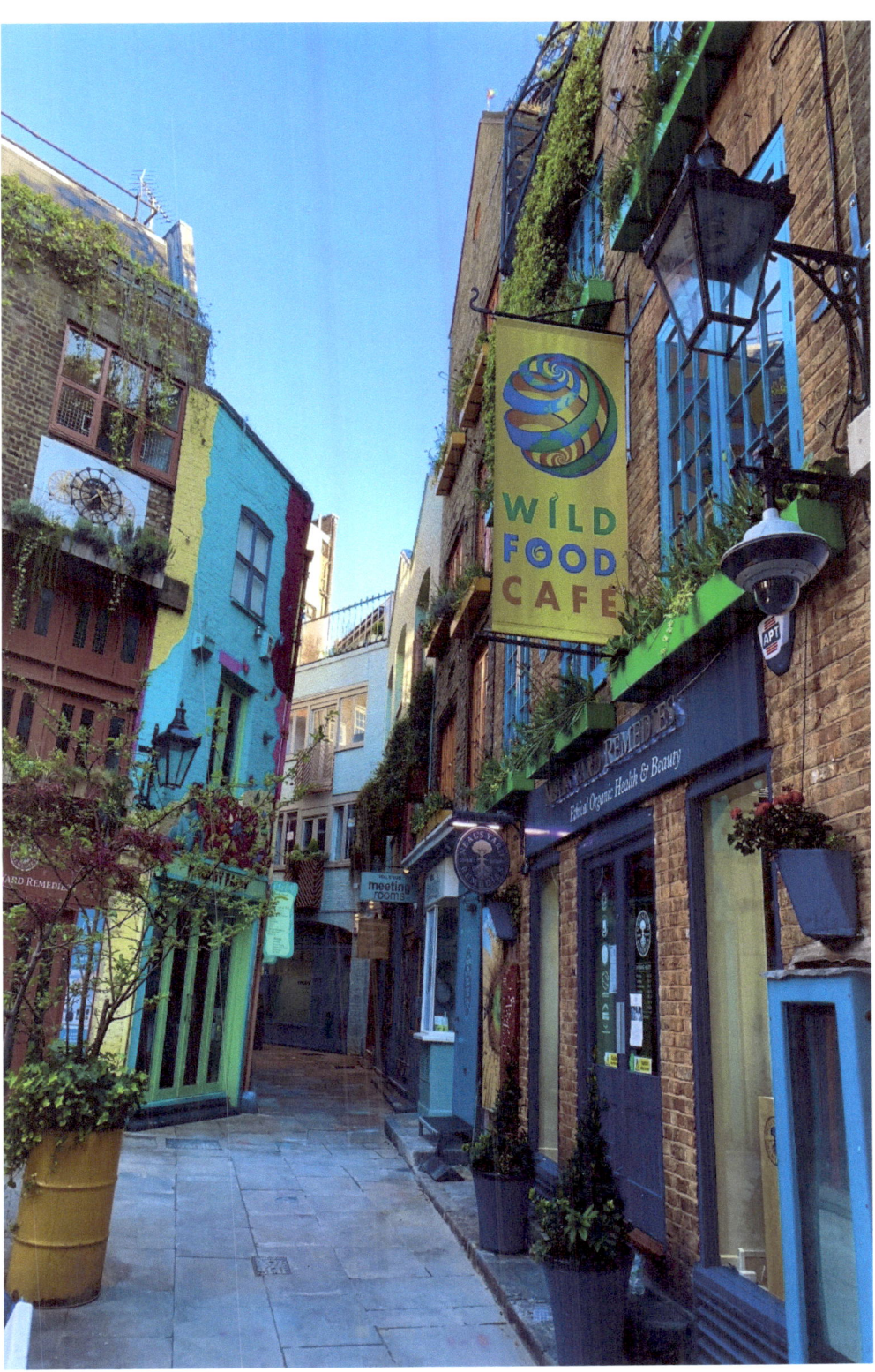

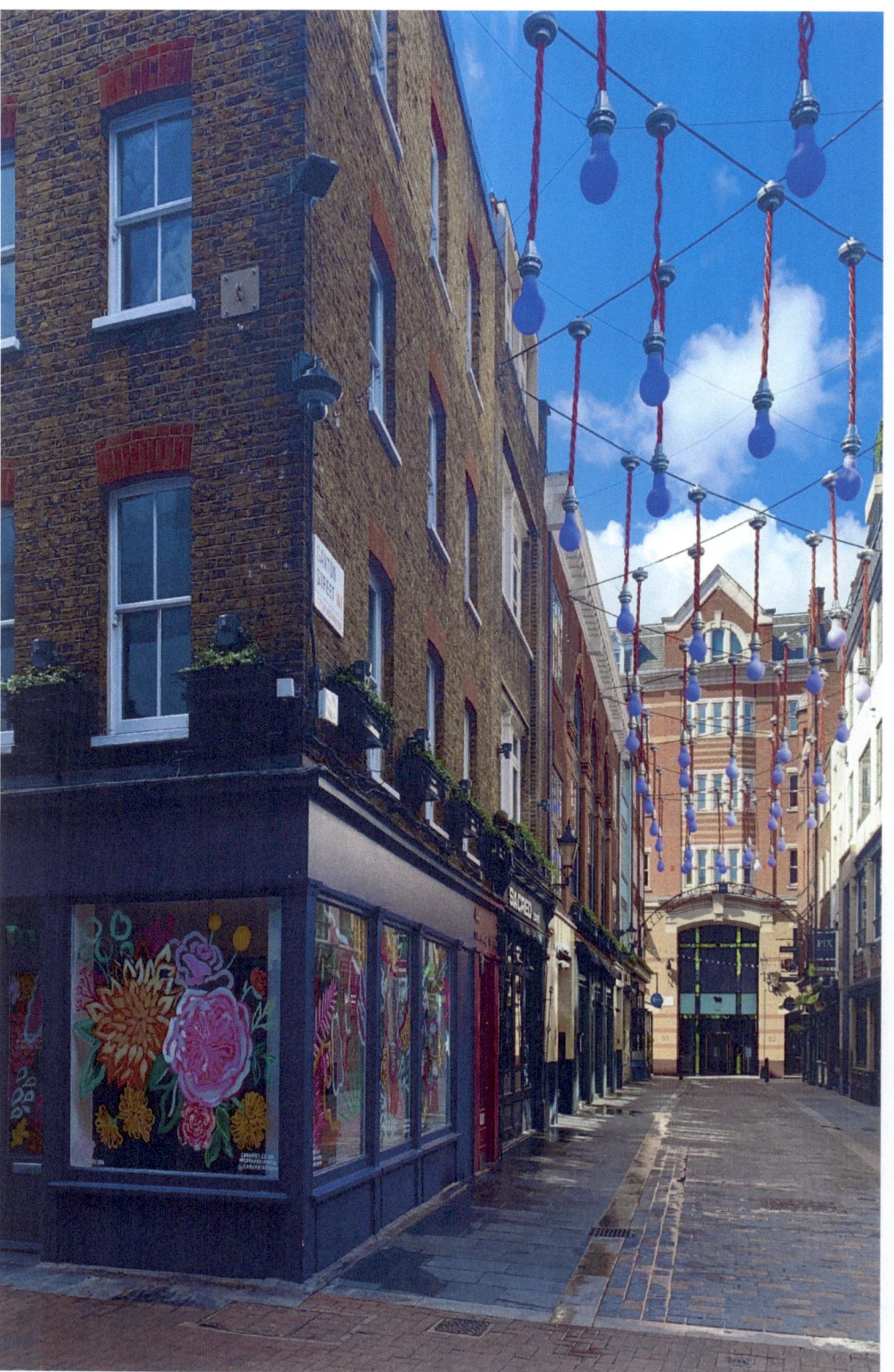

Carnaby Street & Shaftsbury Avenue

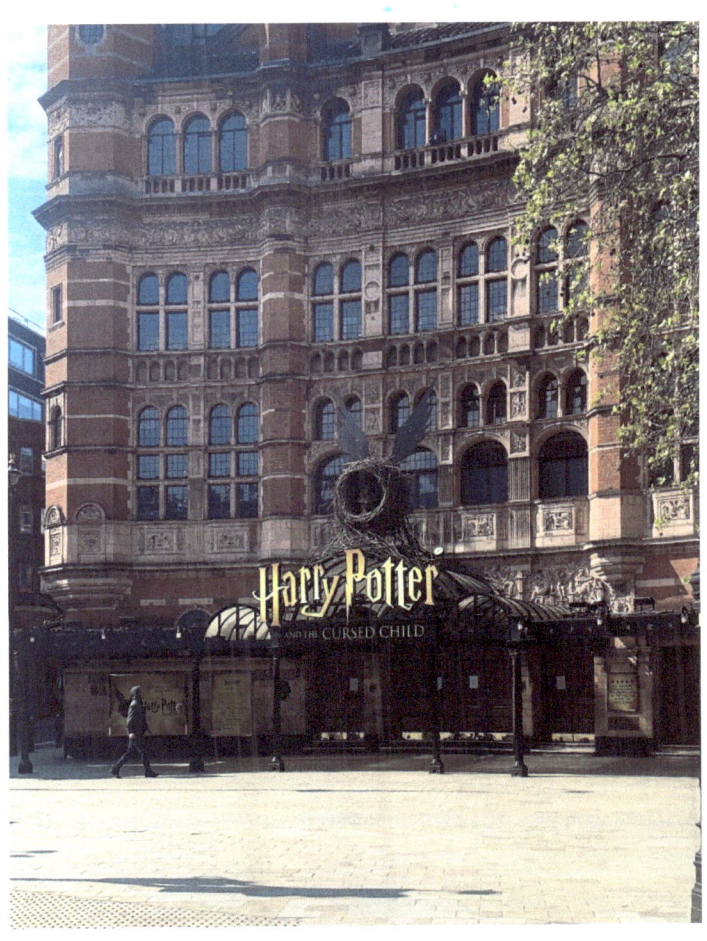

"Train your mind to see the good in everything.
Positivity is a choice"

The Shard

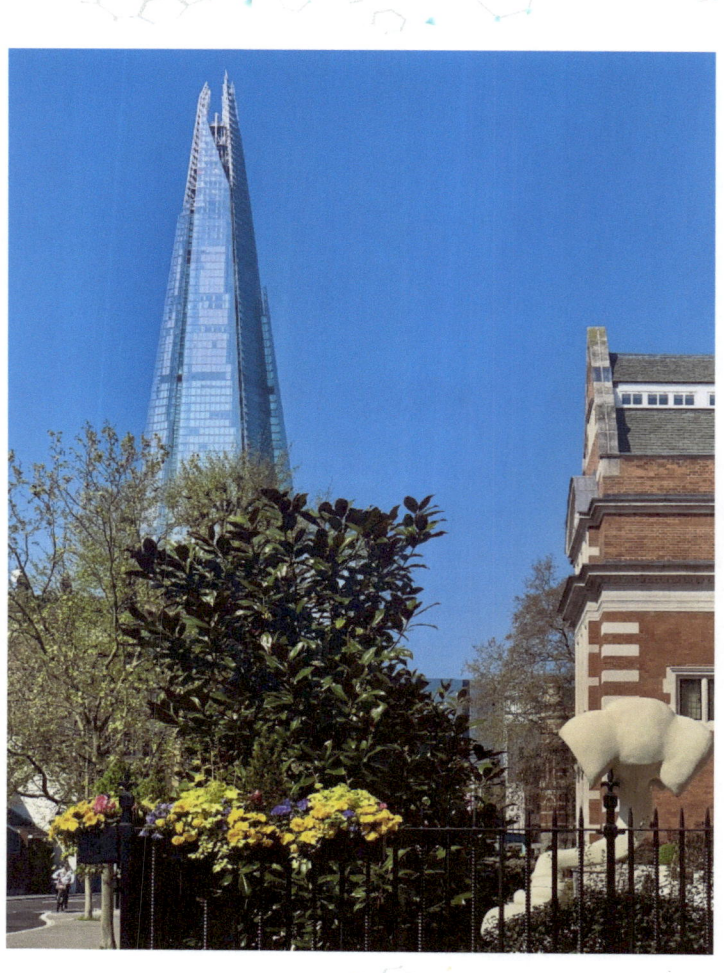

"Positive anything is better than a negative nothing"

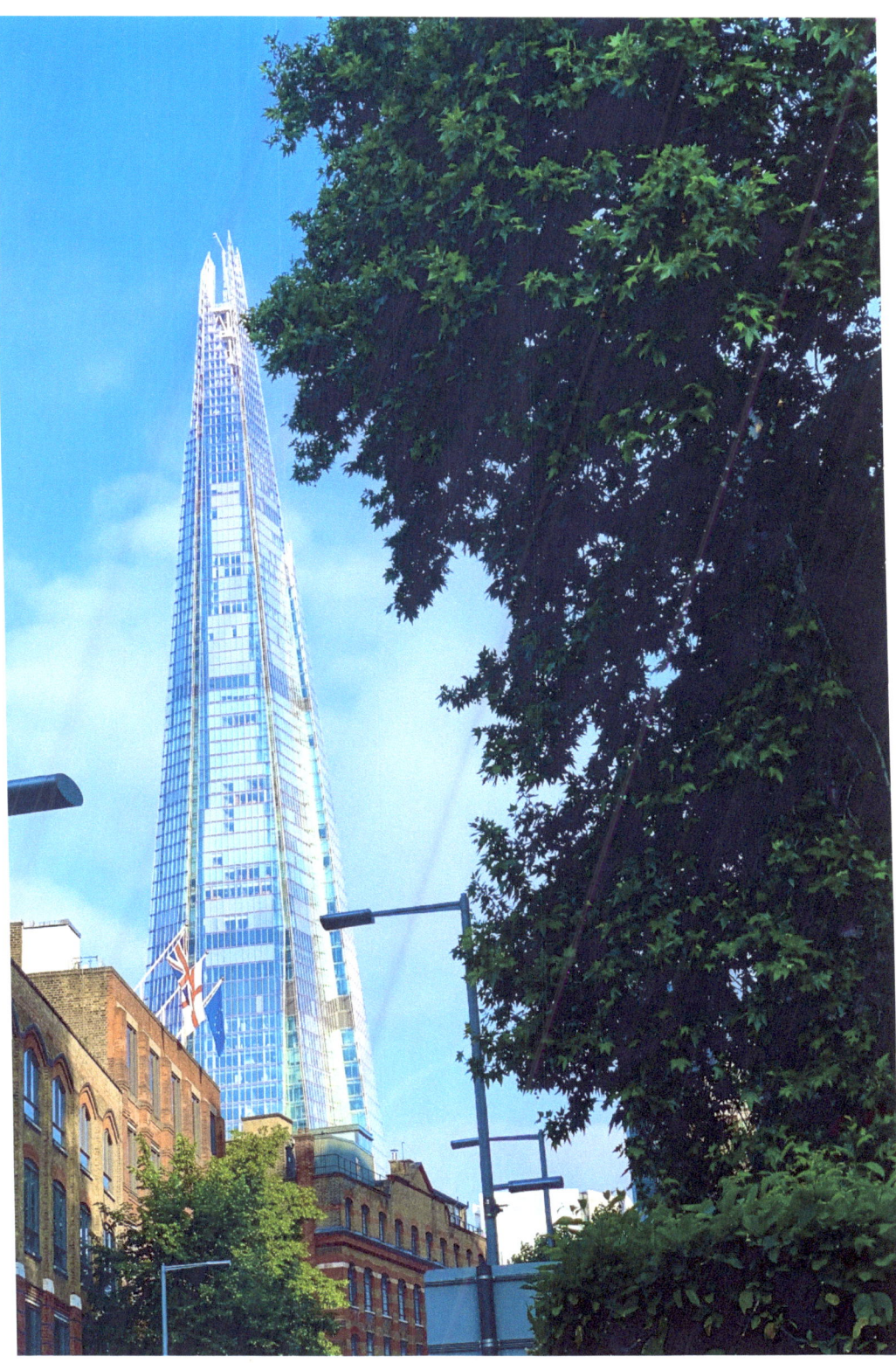

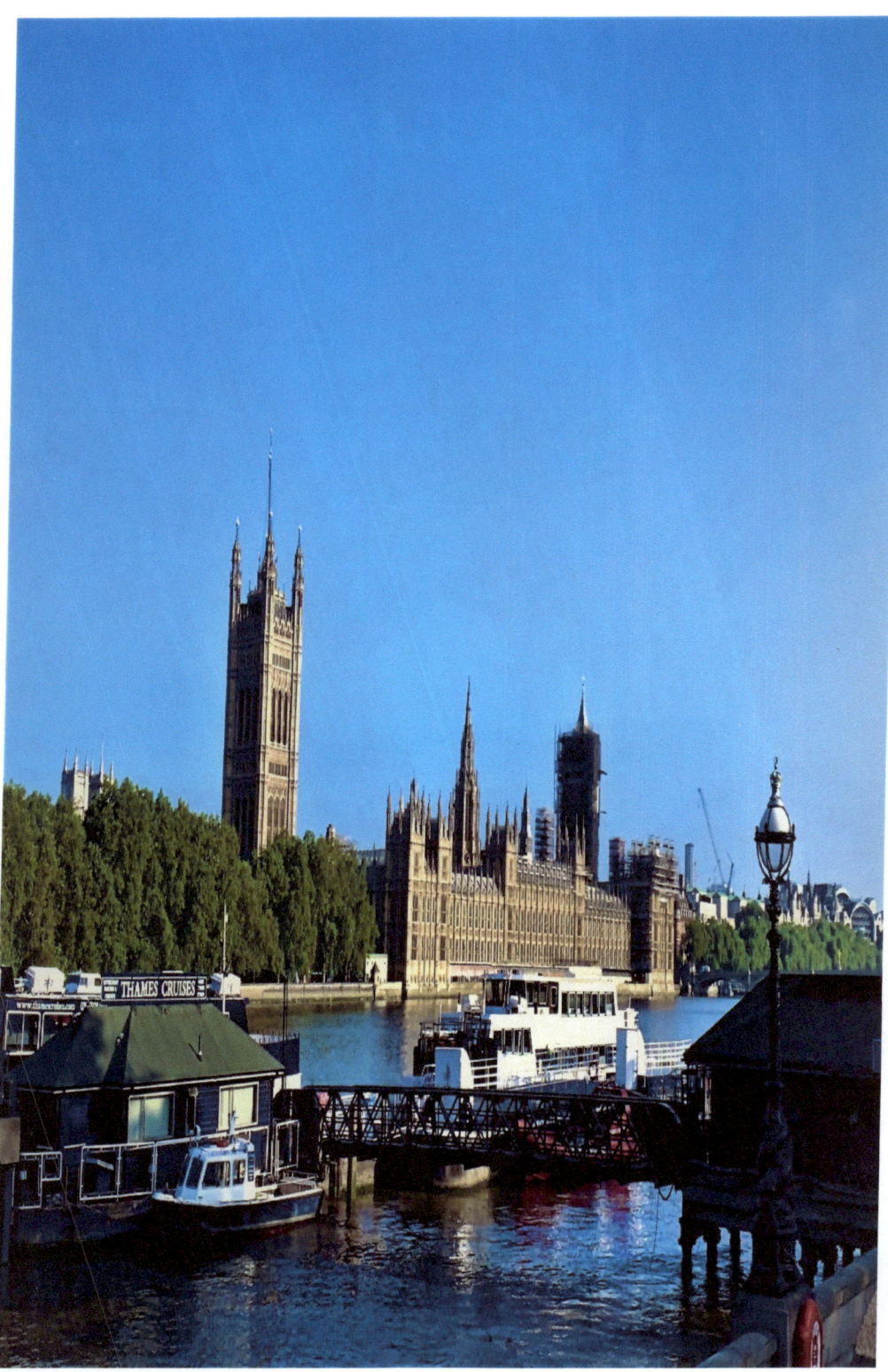

The Thames

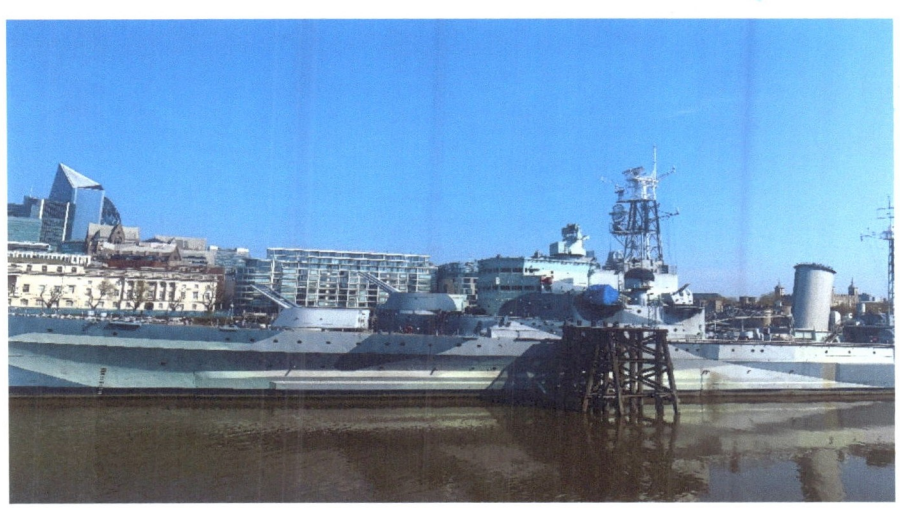

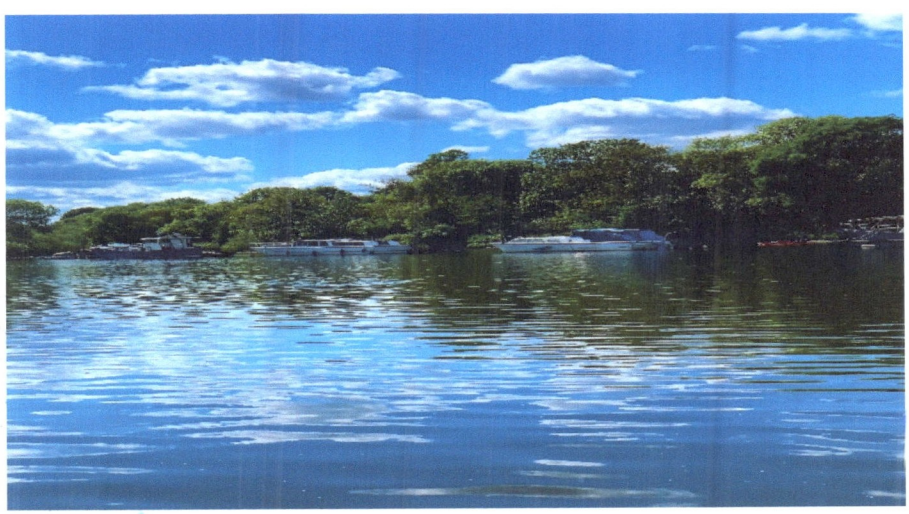

"To be an achiever,
you must start with
being a believer"

TFL (London Underground)

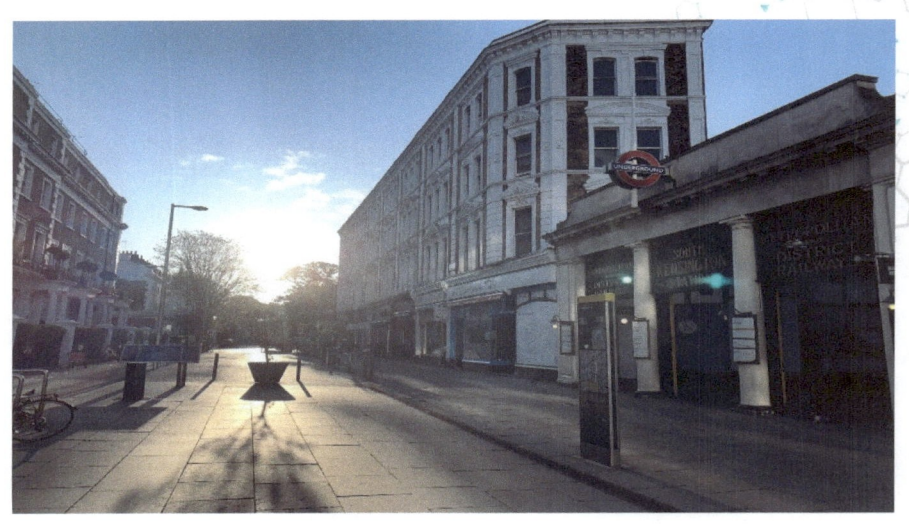

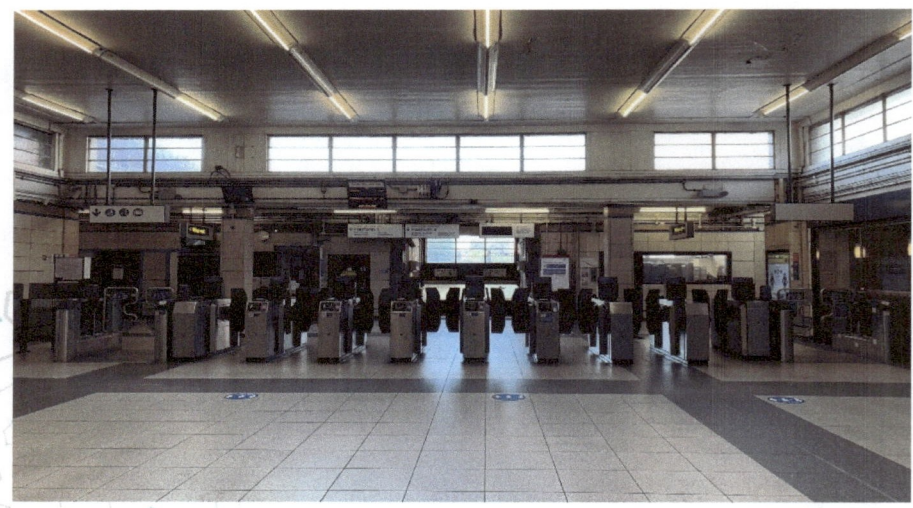

"The best kind of people to be with are kind people"

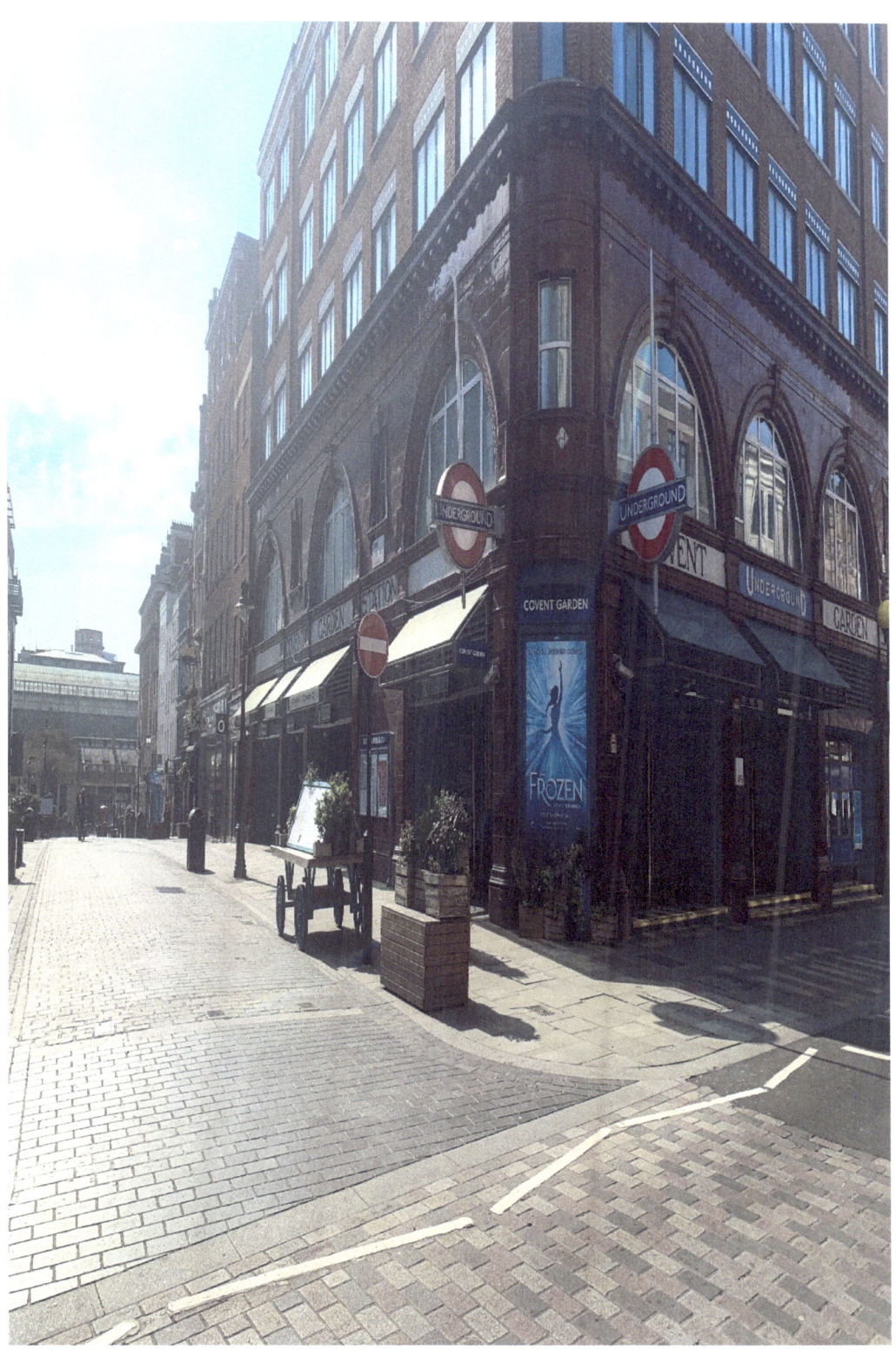

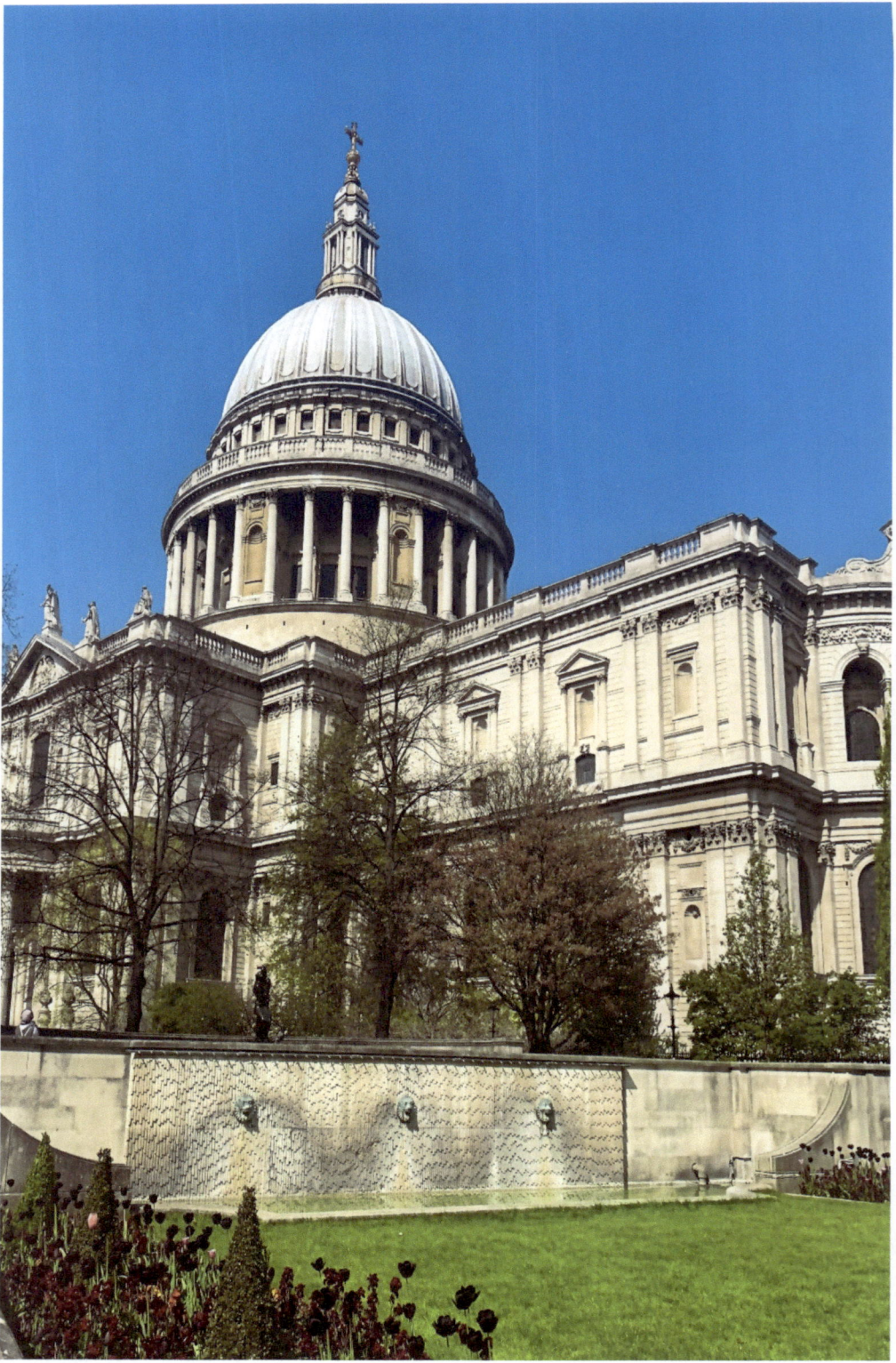

St Paul's Cathedral

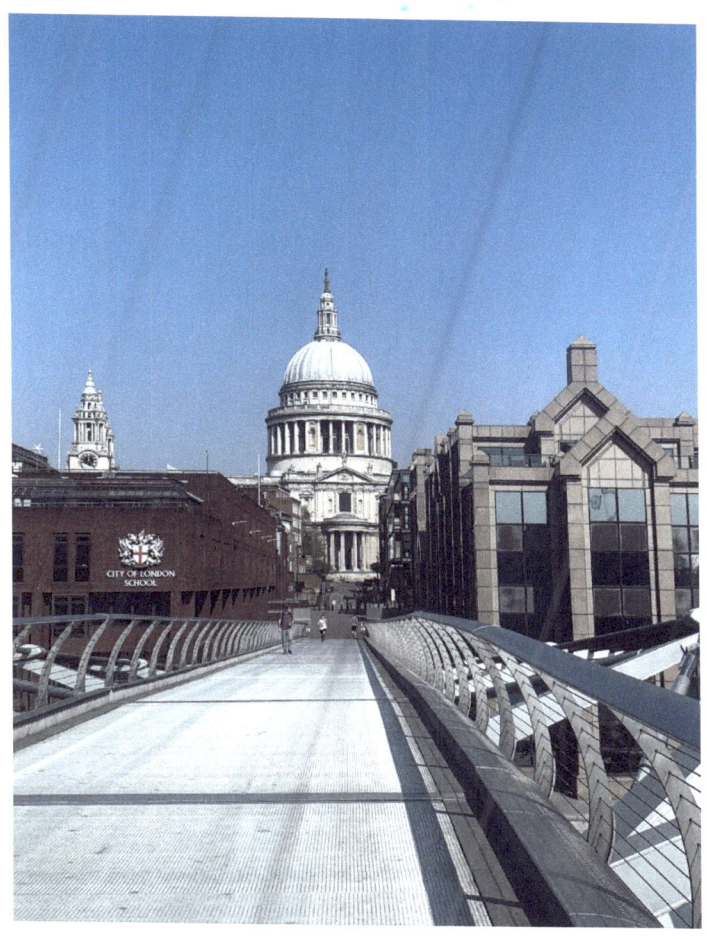

"You should be happy.
Not because everything is good,
but because you can see the good in everything"

The City of London Finance District
& The Royal Court of Justice

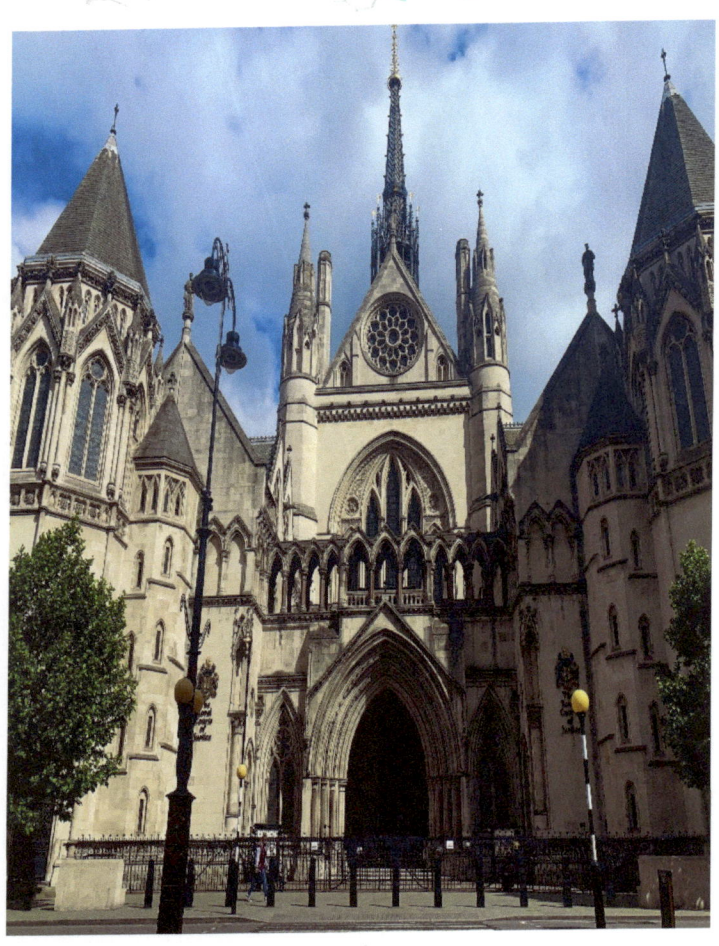

"When the caterpillar thinks
there is no other way,
it turns into a butterfly"

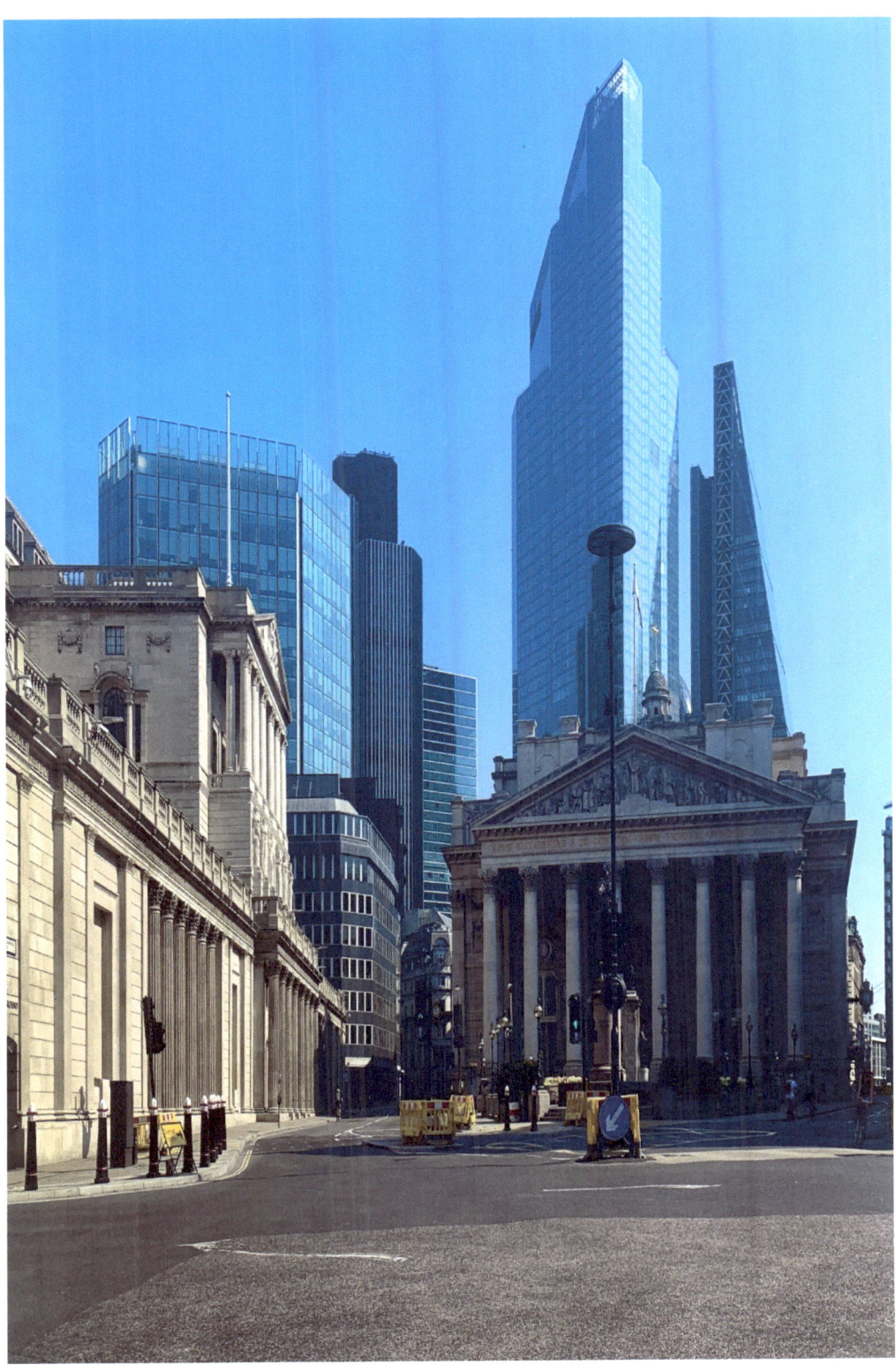

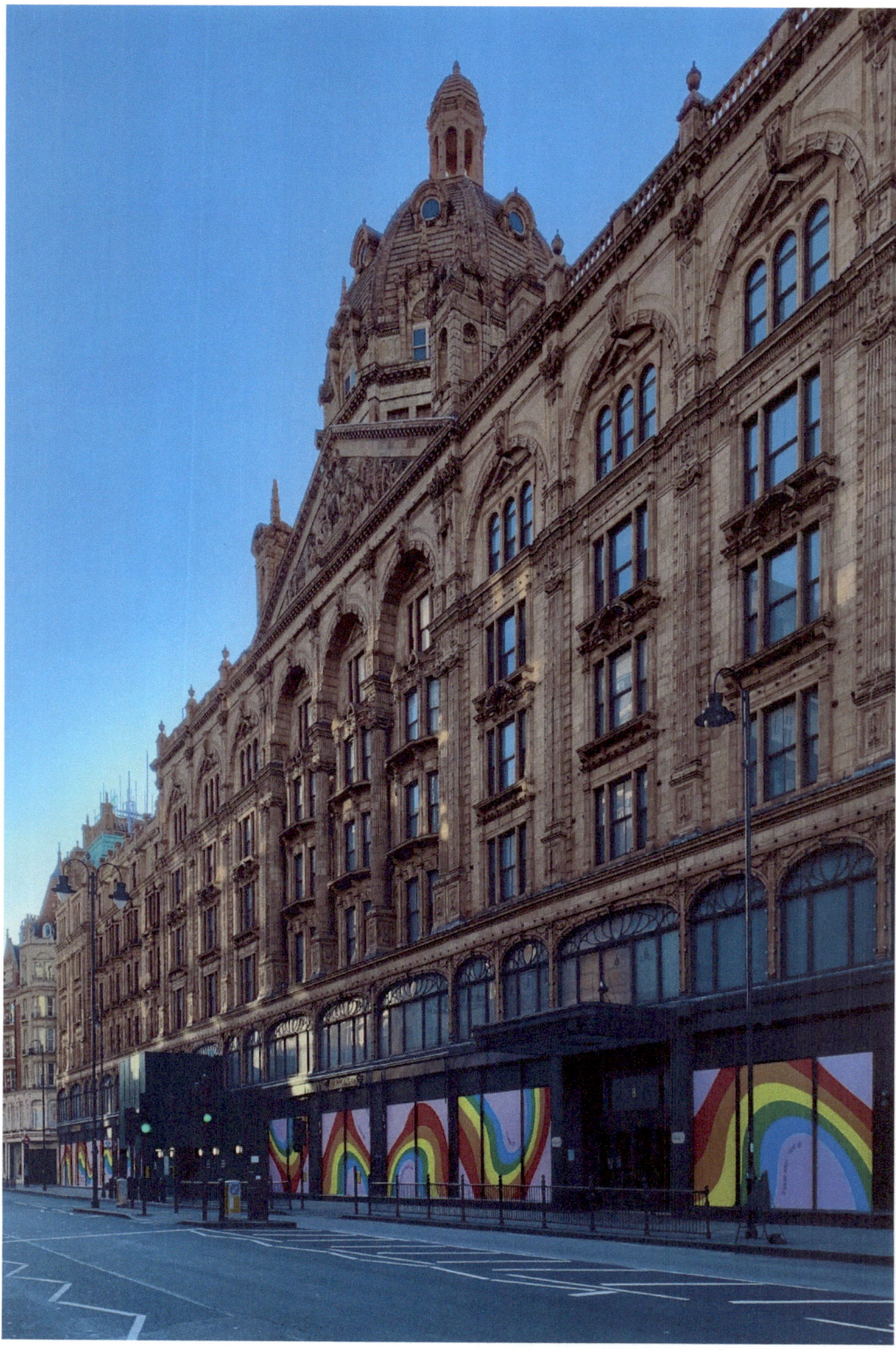

Harrods
Fortnum & Mason

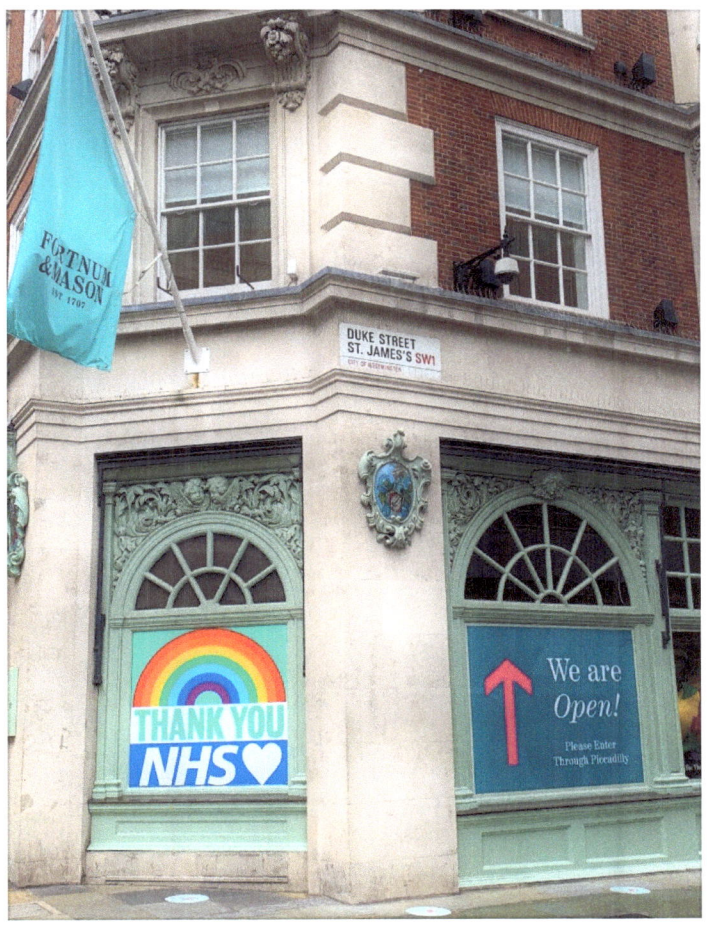

"Do not let negative words live in your head rent free"

St Katherine Docks

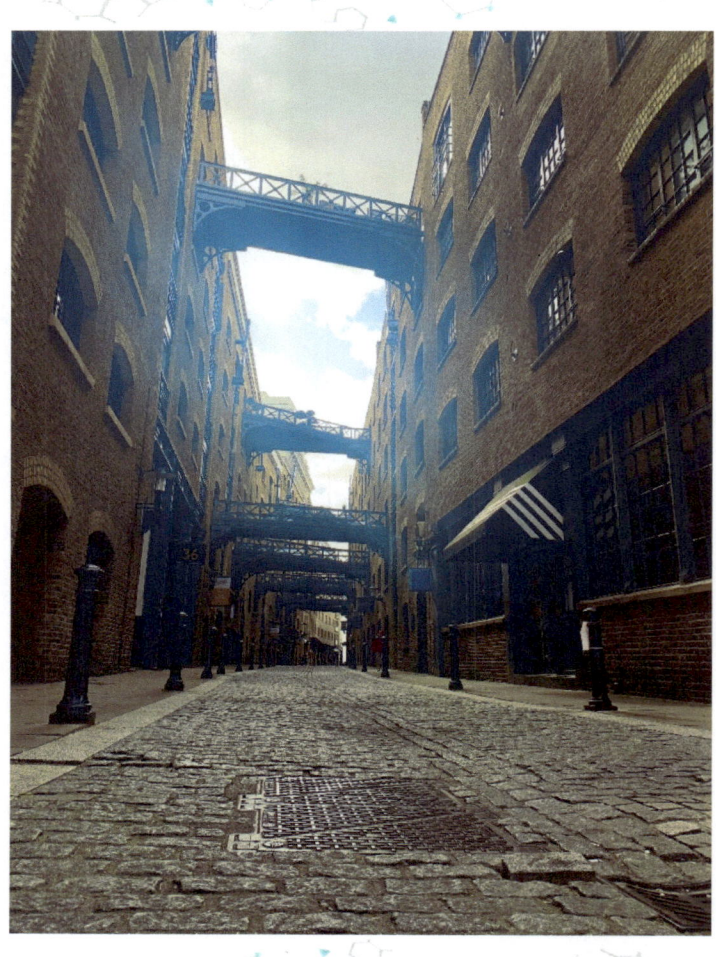

"Things turn out best for the people who make the best of the way things turn out"

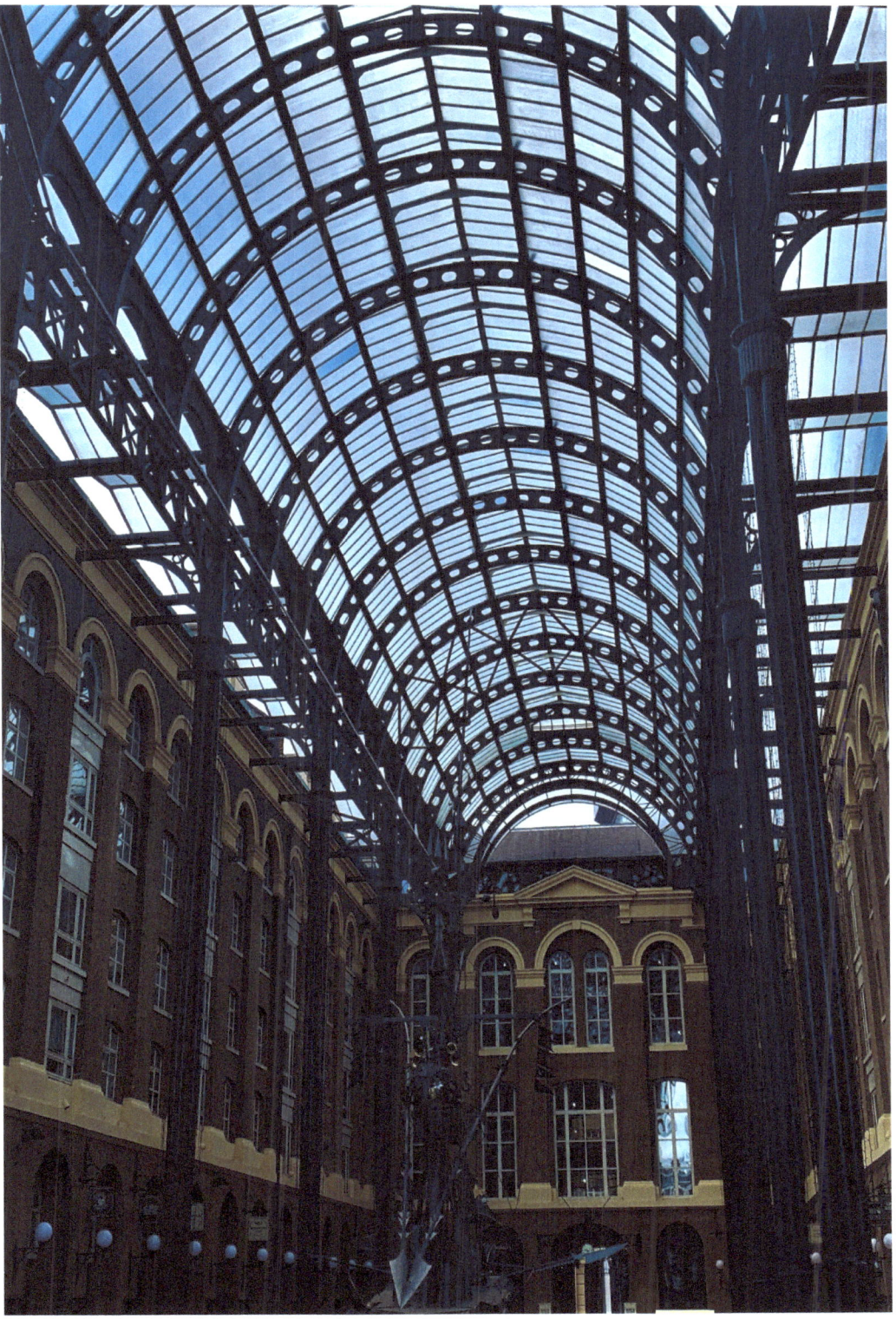

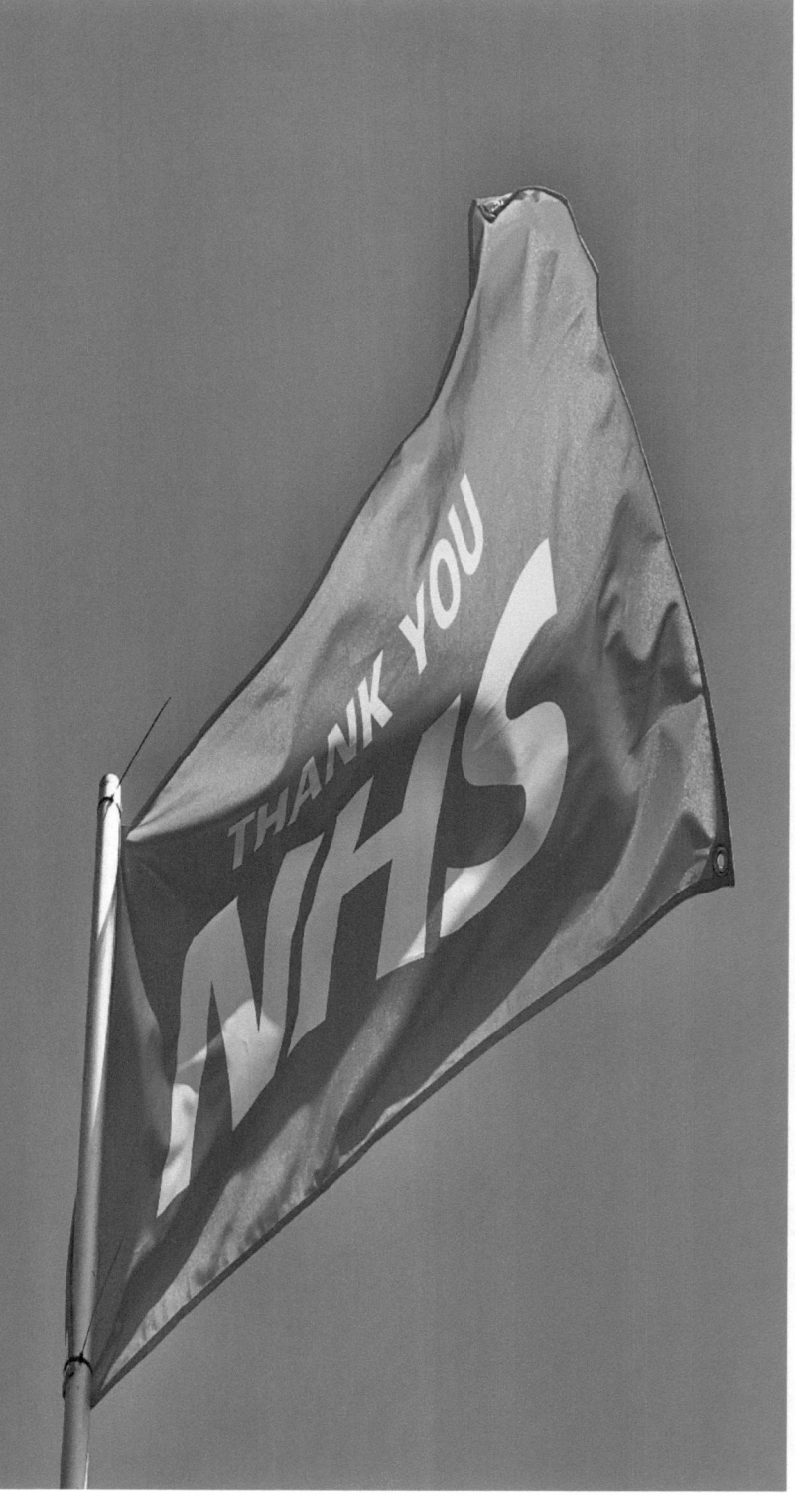

Heroes

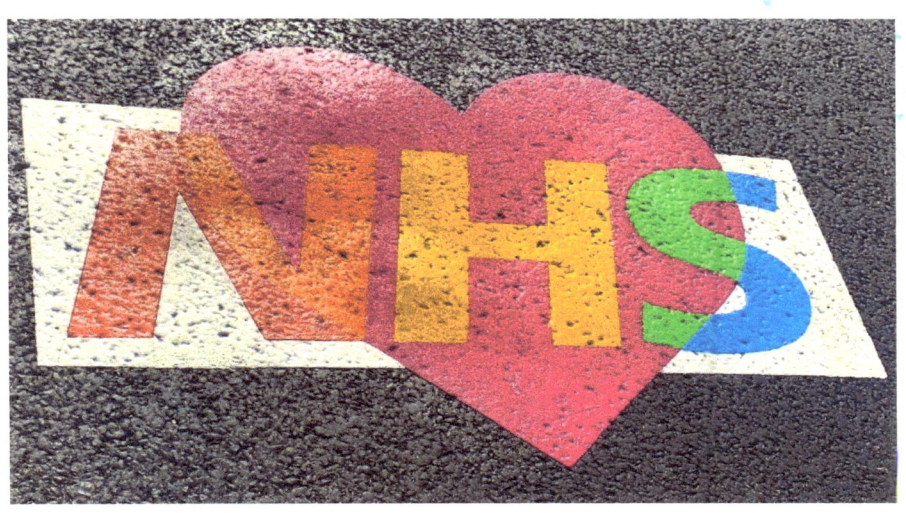

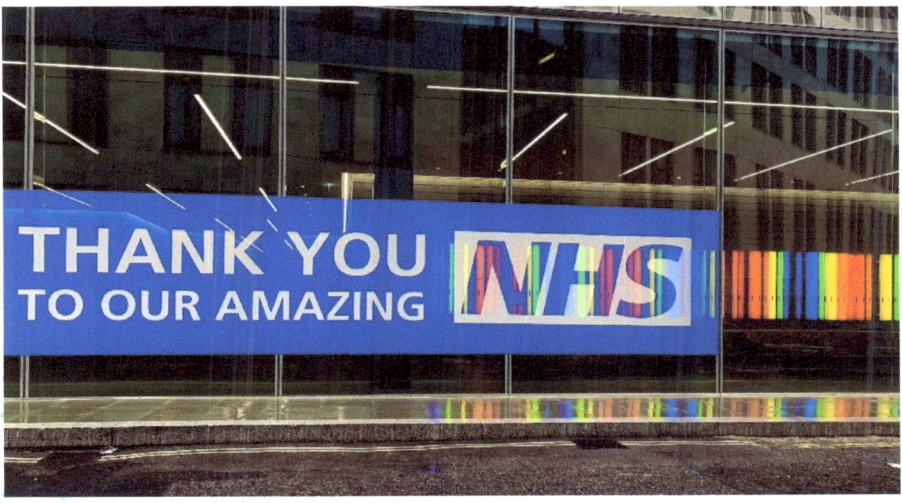

"People of great courage and noble qualities"

Dedication

During COVID-19 I worked within the NHS. I led and implemented care systems and supported clinicians on the front line, all of us working many hours over too many days.

On my first day off, I cycled around London, just aghast with how serene and yet somber it looked. I live in London, so usually avoid such busy chaotic spots, especially on the weekends.

This book is dedicated to all those who work in the NHS in any capacity (including my wife), the teachers and support staff in schools who supported my daughter while we worked tirelessly for this cause.

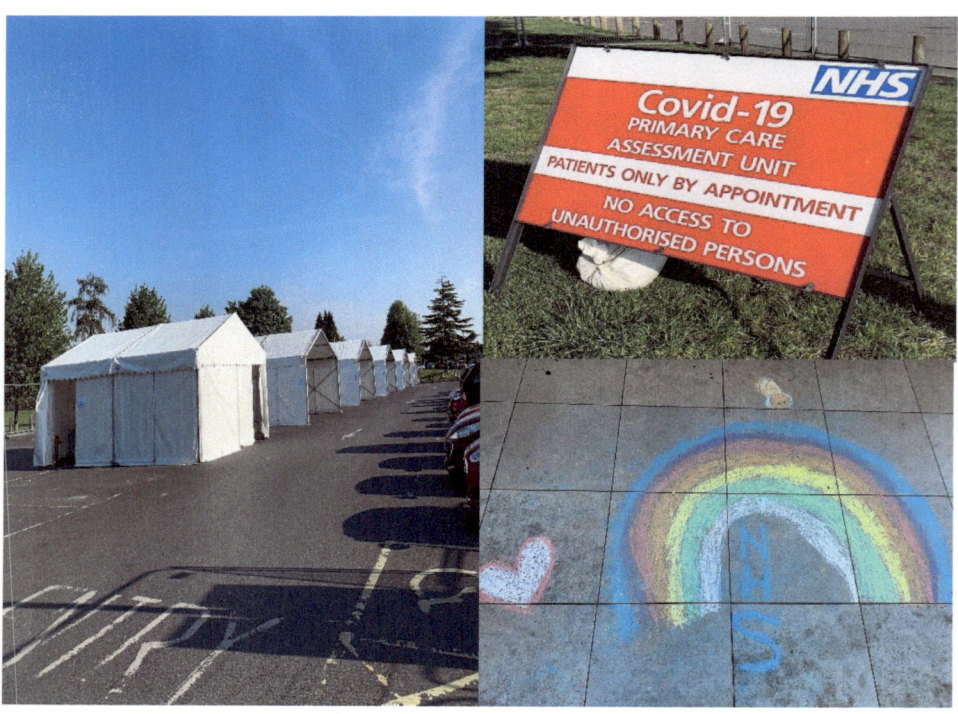

About the author

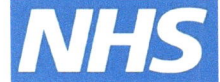 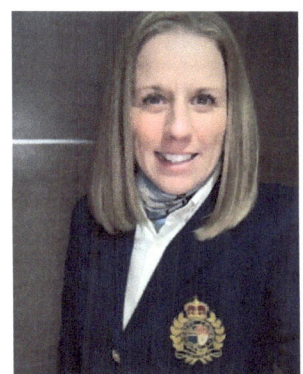 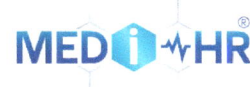

Joanna Fox was a football player in her youth, owing to her competitive spirit, tactical ability to revel in challenges. She has a talent for team ethics, cultivating positive cultures in the workplace and utilising her coaching ability to lead and develop others along the journey.

Her professional passion is people, and aside from the NHS work, she is Managing Director of her own HR consultancy company. She has been in senior management roles for nearly 20 years and is keen to drive improved mental health and wellbeing among the NHS workforce. She believes in the power of continuous learning and holds chartered status.

Aside form that she is blessed with a wonderful family, good humored friends, sound health and fitness and a zest for living her best life. She enjoys photography, reading, cooking/baking, exercise, and quality family time.

www.ingramcontent.com/pod-product-compliance
Lightning Source LLC
Chambersburg PA
CBHW040250220526
45473CB00001B/429